Advance Praise

At the core of this deceptively simple work is Linda Iribarren's abiding faith in the ability
of every individual to meaningfully connect with the deep truths of life. What If You Can Change the World?
offers a compellingly beautiful invitation to intentional living that is utterly accessible to anyone
willing to open these pages and begin the process. What a gift!

— VALERIE THEA VANDERMEER
Founding Director, EarthWalk

Like a well directed arrow, the right questions can help us seek essential truths in our longing to understand ourselves
and our roles in the world. Linda Iribarren clearly understands this, and knows how to encourage a quest through
provocative questions. Her *What If You Can Change The World?* invites us to question our assumptions, look again at our
choices and at our potential to co-create new visions for our planet. This is a book that will gradually be highlighted,
written in the margins and dog-eared because it will be used over and over. I certainly recommend this book.

— GLORIA KARPINSKI,
Author of *Barefoot on Holy Ground*

WOW, Linda Iribarren has forged a creative concept of true rhythm and dance in her series of questions and quotes.
I found the book to flow like a river, and I find that my own 'boulders' make eddies in this stream for me to
contemplate, rearrange my river bed.... so that I can be a better conduit... in the realization of my own "I can do this"
quest. Congratulations for a book that can be picked up at any page for inspiration. I must also add that I really like
the most copious references listings... sources of "fuel" to nourish us and support our quests, as we ride this river of life!

— CHANTAL TOPOROW, PH.D.
Cultivator of Time & Energy,
Aerospace Scientist

When words travel inside us and touch the heart... wisdom opens like a new flower to a warming sun. *What If You Can Change The World?* helps find that magic to inspire.

— LITANY BURNS,
Author of *The Sixth Sense of Children* and *Develop Your Psychic Abilities*

Linda Iribarren's *What if You Can Change the World?* offers a brilliant and soul-uplifting new paradigm educational tool to nurture the rich inner awareness of each person. The deceptively simple *What if Process* is not just a nice "extra," but should be used by every school in America to awaken or recharge the vast creativity and problem-solving capacity available to all persons.

— NANCY BAUMGARTEN, MLA,
Author of *Profound Awareness: Nurturing Creative Genius*,
Director, Enchanted Forest Intuitive Camp

What a lovely book... the kind to keep by your side and just open a page for inspiration, or to discover new direction for your life.

— SUSAN GALE,
A Place of Light, and co-author of *Edgar Cayce on the Indigo Children*

WHAT IF YOU CAN CHANGE THE WORLD?

ACCESSING ANSWERS TO THE QUESTIONS OF LIFE

Radiant Star
PUBLISHING
Carlton

LINDA IRIBARREN

The material contained in this book is not intended as medical advice. Contact a qualified physician if you have a medical issue or illness.

Copyright permissions on page 271.

Book design by 1106 Design.

First edition published 2005.

Radiant Star PUBLISHING   P. O. Box 160, Carlton, WA 98814-0160
www.radiantstarpublishing.com

ISBN 0-9726112-0-7 Hardcover

Library of Congress Control Number: 2004097969

Printed in the United States of America

Publisher's Cataloging-in-Publication
(Provided by Quality Books, Inc.)

    Iribarren, Linda.
      What if you can change the world? : accessing answers
    to the questions of life / Linda Iribarren. — 1st ed.
      p. cm.
      Includes bibliographical references.
      LCCN 2004097969
      ISBN 0-9726112-0-7

      1. Self-actualization (Psychology) 2. Spirituality.
    I. Title.

    BF637.S4I75 2005   158.1
                     QBI04-700559

Table of Contents

Acknowledgments

With deep gratitude, I would like to thank each of you who blessed me with your support, and assistance. While appreciative of each one of you, and for everything you provided, I owe special thanks to a few people in particular.

To Robin and Jim, for your continuous encouragement. Without you both, this book would never have been published.

To Llael Maffitt, for your love and insights, so willingly shared.

To Tobin Hart, for your wisdom, integrity, open heart, and most especially, for the gift of profound words you so graciously provided.

To Kathleen Hirschstein, for your editing, and suggestions. Any mistakes are mine alone, and not a result of your advice.

To Nancy Baumgarten, for your unwavering friendship, and continuous offers of help.

To Valerie Vandermeer, for your boundless enthusiasm, and insightful critiques.

To Michele DeFilippo, for your creative expression, collaborative style, and handholding.

To my community and extended family, for all that you are, and all that you do, frequently without even knowing of your contributions. You exemplify kindness, support and generosity.

To Ric, for all you provided, and all you relinquished, so that I could create this gift from my heart.

This book was birthed out

of the love and compassion shared

with two extraordinary friends,

Bill and Jim

THE
FOREWORD

Contemplate the workings of this world, listen to the words of the wise, and take all that is good as your own. With this as your base, open your own door to truth.

~Morihei Ueshiba

This is a book that is designed to open possibility.

Seeing before believing is the credo of modern science. We are encouraged to believe something only after we see it for ourselves. For the most part, this works just fine, providing the kind of verification that helps us avoid foolishness and superstition. However, when it comes to spiritual matters, it is sometimes necessary to believe *before* we can see. More precisely, this means suspending *disbelief* in order to open ourselves to whatever is before us. This does not mean abandoning our critical mind or being a naïve convert to some idea or doctrine; rather, it means turning off our critical judgment for a moment in order to open up to possibility. I think this is the meaning of faith. And what faith does is build a bridge between the known and the unknown that allows us to cross into new possibility—it opens our consciousness and allows us to see the invisible and do the impossible. I am reminded of the transformation of an old friend of mine at the hands of possibility.

As he entered high school, Hugh was a troubled and troubling underachiever. He was on the fast track to a disappointing life. However, his school had an unusual experiment at the time that involved periodically bussing Hugh and a group of his peers to the nearby Princeton University campus, where students listened to presentations by distinguished physicists of the day, Einstein among them. The hope was that these scientists might have a positive impact on the lives of these difficult teens.

One day, after a long, dry talk by one of the physicists, a young girl sitting in the back of the lecture hall raised her hand and wryly asked these men of science what they thought of ghosts. After some chuckles, the first physicist stood up and with clear and definite certainty entirely dismissed any possibility of their existence. When he was done, the second scientist took his turn and with great authority rejected any chance of there being ghosts and cited a lack of any hard scientific evidence. When they had finished, Robert Oppenheimer, who was instrumental in the development of the atomic bomb and then the staunchest opponent of its use, took his turn. He stood up, paused for a moment, and said, "That's a fascinating question. I accept the possibility of all things," and he went on to say that "it is necessary to find one's own required evidence before accepting or rejecting a possibility."

For Hugh, this moment was a moment of revelation that forever changed his life. Instead of closing down and accepting the world as prepackaged, Oppenheimer's perspective opened it back up to mystery, to the possibility of all things, and to one's responsibility to discover and find truth for oneself. Hugh's inner life began a monumental shift as he came to define himself from the center of his own direct experience rather than shutting down to conform to what others said was real or true. Hugh went on to become a distinguished, innovative, and also irreverent teacher who helped open up possibilities for others, including me. This moment helped him to believe so that he could see. And that's just where this book has the power to move us to, to the possibility of all things.

Yet this is not a book that provides answers so much as one that offers questions. Questions have a power beyond any immediate answers they may imply. Questions are the fuel for the pursuit of wisdom. Wisdom seeks questions, as if looking for the best fruit on the tree. It then bites into the question, feeling it, living it, and allowing it to fulfill its purpose as nourishment. Whereas intelligence will cut, dismantle, and reconstruct the question in order to work toward certainty, wisdom rides the question to see where it goes and what it opens into.

And like the sacred texts of the wisdom traditions this is a book of *living words*. These questions, these words are compressed or encrypted data. They are the surface and the symbol of deeper knowing that is revealed only according to the quality of our awareness. How are these words "unstuffed," how is the code broken, how do we unwrap the gift? In order to open the words we must allow ourselves to be opened by them. This is like a key opening a series of locks that leads simultaneously into our Selves and into the words. This is what the Sufis call *knowledge by presence*—a process of uncoiling the mystical data that has been encrypted in words.

This is a book from the heart of joy. I suspect you have had moments where some special words seemed to resonate right down to your soul? Maybe an insight became crystal clear or your heart popped open. Plato called this knowing *anamnesis*—the soul's remembrance of truth. That's what this deceivingly simple book offers. It is a special invitation by a *joy-master*—a wise soul who understands the power of possibility and lives from the center of joy.

May you find nourishment here.

Tobin Hart, Ph.D.

Author, *The Secret Spiritual World of Children, From Information to Transformation,* and *Transpersonal Knowing*

THE
INTRODUCTION

You are a tiny world within yourself.
When there is peace, harmony, love and
understanding right there deep within
your little world, it will be reflected in
the outer world all around you.

~Eileen Caddy

Do you want to make a difference? Does your heart yearn to know how? Are you searching for your specific purpose, your service? Are you seeking answers?

To find answers, don't you usually begin with questions?

"In all affairs it's a healthy thing now and then to hang a question mark on the things you have long taken for granted" Bertrand Russell advises, and Indira Gandhi proclaims that "The power to question is the basis of all human progress."

I realized the beauty and power of questions while searching for a way to help a friend discover his own truth before passing over. I could physically feel a stirring in my heart, and the sensation of a flower opening its petals, one by one. Compassion, powerfully awakened, poured questions onto paper in service to my friend. Those original questions have multiplied and have been fine-tuned, and are offered now in service to you in finding *your* truth, *your* answers.

Each of us has our own unique perspective, our own base assumptions about the nature of reality that determines our worldview. In our diversity lies great wealth; indeed even our differences help us recognize the full potential of our being. We also have much in common, starting with the very essence of our being, which is love. The synergy of our combined energies can empower a vision of existence that is harmonious and inclusive, that transforms old ways into new insights, and that fosters peace, compassion, wisdom, and joy.

Answers exist inside each of us, ready and waiting to be accessed; ready to add value to our lives. The key that opens the door to all the answers we seek is personal experience. It allows us to leap beyond our reliance on input from outside ourselves to direct knowing that is undeniable, to process from the inside out.

In daily life, we generate thoughts and feelings as we experience each situation that occurs. Wisdom results from thinking with our hearts and feeling with our minds. It's the integration of the two that provides a balanced platform for discovery, a unitive perspective that honors both thoughts and feelings. And, wisdom is a state of being available to everyone. Yet we have been raised to focus almost exclusively on our thoughts, with limited information available to assist us with the purpose and usefulness of emotions.

Feelings are incredible blessings. Feelings open us to the possibility of transformation; they are the secret power that resides right out in the open. They show us how our choices create our experiences, provide feedback about what is meaningful to us, point out our beliefs and biases, and show us where we direct our attention. Emotions are powerful catalysts energizing our thoughts into physical manifestation so that we can remember who we are, and our purpose for being here now.

Feelings express through our bodies, continually giving us direct input. "There is constant communication between mind and body" states Shakti Gawain. "The body perceives the physical universe, and sends messages to the mind about it; the mind interprets the perceptions according to its own individual past experience and its belief system, and signals the body to react in a way which it feels appropriate." Intuitively, we often know the messages our bodies are providing. Sometimes we just need to ask, to be curious about what it is we need to understand, or do. Louise Hay believes "The body is always talking to us, if we will only take the time to listen."

Wonder at the perfection of it; the very instrument we need to interpret the data we receive is that which houses our divinity. Our body is that instrument, and it's with us anytime, anywhere. Gregg Braden delivers the message that "Shifting your body chemistry by shifting your viewpoint is perhaps the single most powerful tool that you have available to you for the remainder of your life." What you shift, how and when you choose to do it, is up to you. It's important to keep what's working, and become aware of what is not. Isn't that the information we need to make good choices?

I invite you to read through this book once; to satisfy your curiosity. Then read it again, slowly, allowing plenty of time to savor each page, to absorb all that is available. You may find yourself flipping through a few questions not pertinent right now; only to be stopped by the next as you enter into what Abraham Maslow called a "peak experience." You could be thrust beyond the confines of the ordinary into a moment of joyful insight, transformative in nature. You may walk away, only to be 'called back' by a specific question. Any strong emotion is an indication that the question has something to offer you in the present. You may spend hours, days or even weeks on a single question that is particularly significant to you. While there is value in reading each page sequentially, let intuition be your guide.

Your direct experience is enhanced by using the *What if* Process with each and every question. Doing so can open doors you didn't even realize were closed. It is easy to use and specifically designed for discovery, and for verification. It empowers you to be in charge, to explore your thoughts and feelings at your own pace, and to determine the depth of your exploration. You may elect to read the book numerous times, because each time you read the questions again, use the process again, a new revelation can occur.

You have the ability to discover through direct experience the sweetness of *knowing*, to reclaim the profound awareness that is your birthright.

Your answers are the story of your own becoming.

THE
WHAT IF PROCESS

My beliefs I test on my body, on my intuitional consciousness, and when I get a response there, then I accept.

~D. H. Lawrence

The What if Process

As you read each *What if You Can Change the World?* question, pay attention to both your thoughts and your feelings. Approach each question with a sense of curiosity, as an opportunity for learning something new about yourself, for realizing personal potential.

Try the perspective of each question on as you would a new piece of clothing. What if such and such is true? What would that concept mean if applied to your life as you live it now? Notice what you think about it. Notice what you feel. You may begin to process with a simple "ah ha," "of course," or "no way." Pay attention to any questions that arise, any insights you have. Allow yourself to follow associations, as they are linked by emotions. The more feeling, the more intense the associative link, so if you're having strong emotions of any kind, great!

Just as you would look at your reflection in a mirror checking out different angles, do the same with your daily existence. Use your daily life as the mirror providing feedback as you try on the perspective of each question. Notice any shifts in attitude, new feelings expressing themselves, new thoughts arising as you "try on" the view the questions evoke. If you don't like the new perspective, if it doesn't fit, then just as you would select a different piece of clothing to try on, select a different belief or stay with the one that you already had, one that is working for you.

Listening to your body is an easy way to learn what your emotions are trying to communicate. Each feeling produces a physical sensation in your body. Allow yourself to jump into the flow of your feelings without suppressing or controlling them, and see what they reveal to you. Becoming mindful of where feeling energy is located helps you access useful information about yourself, and the pattern of feelings can assist you in more clearly understanding your response to situations, events and relationships. It is easy to access personalized answers once you know how to recognize the clues your own body provides in each moment.

Your insights may be subtle initially. You may experience sensations you are more accustomed to, like butterflies in the stomach or chills running around. Be gentle with yourself, this is something new. We each have our own style, our own unique method of accessing our inner self. Trust your process, it is perfect for you!

For maximum benefit, journal as you process. Doing so will provide you a great deal of data for further insights later, in recognizing associations not immediately apparent.

Most importantly, enjoy!

THE QUESTIONS

I have learned, as a rule of thumb, never
to ask whether you can do something.
Say, instead, that you are doing it.
Then fasten your seat belt. The most
remarkable things follow.

~Julia Cameron

What if

you can change

the world?

This world is but a canvas
to our imagination.

~Henry David Thoreau

anything you

can imagine

is possible?

Destiny is not a matter of chance,
but of choice.

~William Jennings Bryan

What if

you have the

power of choice?

It is not the strongest of the species that survive, nor the most intelligent, but the one most responsive to change.

~Charles Darwin

What if

when you

realize you

have choices,

you choose

differently?

The real voyage of discovery
consists not in seeking new lands
but seeing with new eyes.

~Marcel Proust

What if

change exists in

every moment?

Change is the nursery of music,
joy, life and Eternity.

~John Donne

change allows

awareness

to develop?

All appears to change when we change.

~Henri Amiel

What if

you choose how

change manifests

in your life?

Life is a sum of all your choices.

~Albert Camus

What if

not choosing is a

choice in itself?

To exist is to change;
To change is to mature;
To mature is to create oneself endlessly.

~Henri Bergson

you can

create changes

with fear,

or with love?

Love is the source out of
which being comes.

~Jane Roberts

What if

love is the fabric

of your being?

Fear is static that prevents me
from hearing myself.

~Samuel Butler

fear is a learned

response?

What I believe is a process
rather than a finality.

~Emma Goldman

your beliefs

determine

your fears?

Whatever the event, you are its origin.

~Maggid of Mezeritch

you attract that

which you fear?

When fear is present, wisdom cannot be.

~Lucius C. Lactantius

you energize the

things you resist?

Come to the edge
We can't, we are afraid
Come to the edge
We can't, we will fall
And they came to the edge
And he pushed them
And they flew.

~Guillaume Apollinaire

What if

resistance

indicates a

self-limiting

belief?

Tension is who you think you should be.
Relaxation is who you are.

~Chinese proverb

stress delivers

direct feedback?

Nothing in life is to be feared.
It is only to be understood.

~Marie Curie

What if

fear provides

valuable

information?

As we're liberated from our own fear, our presence automatically liberates others.

~Marianne Williamson

What if

you can choose

to appreciate

fear as a great

teacher?

Search thine own heart. What paineth
thee in others in thyself may be.

~John Greenleaf Whittier

What if

fear can

express itself

as anger,

judgment

or pain?

What lies behind us and what lies before us are tiny matters compared to what lies within us.

~Ralph Waldo Emerson

What if

anger is birthed

from a lack of

self-worth?

Self-awareness—recognizing a feeling
as it happens—is the keystone of
emotional intelligence.

~Daniel Goleman

What if self-esteem is

enhanced by

emotional

awareness?

In my life's chain of events nothing was accidental. Everything happened according to an inner need.

~Hannah Senesh

What if

everything

happens for

a purpose?

I am the master of my fate:
I am the captain of my soul.

~W. E. Henley

there are

no victims?

The crisis is to be regarded
as a nexus of growth.

~Jacob Burckhardt

What if

crises create

opportunities

for expanding

awareness?

To overcome difficulties is to experience
the full delight of existence.

~*Arthur Schopenhauer*

What if

dilemmas

offer impetus

for greater

fulfillment?

I cannot believe that the inscrutable
universe turns on an axis of suffering;
surely the strange beauty of the world
must somewhere rest on pure joy!

~Louise Bogan

suffering isn't

necessary?

He suffers more than is necessary,
who suffers before it is necessary.

~*Seneca the Younger*

What if

suffering exists

when you think

situations are

permanent?

Compassion is the keen awareness of
the interdependence of all things.

~*Thomas Merton*

What if

awareness

of suffering

generates

compassion?

If you maintain a feeling of compassion, loving kindness, then something automatically opens your inner door. Through that, you can communicate much more easily with other people. And that feeling of warmth creates a kind of openness. You'll find that all human beings are just like you, so you'll be able to relate to them more easily.

~Bstan-'dzin-rgya-mtsho, Dalai Lama XIV

What if

compassion

tempers the

need to judge?

Out beyond ideas of wrongdoing
and rightdoing, there is a field.
I'll meet you there.

~Jalai Ud-Din Rumi

placing blame

reinforces guilt?

I've learned from experience that the greater part of our happiness or misery depends on our dispositions and not on our circumstances.

~Martha Washington

guilt is just

a lesson not

yet learned?

When one is a stranger to oneself, then one is estranged from others, too.

~Anne Morrow Lindbergh

What if

issues are about

you, rather than

about others?

He drew a circle that shut me out—
Heretic, rebel, a thing to flout.
But Love and I had the wit to win:
We drew a circle that took him in!

~Edwin Markham

What if

no one has

to be wrong

for you to

be right?

To be what we are and to become
what we are capable of becoming
is the only end of life.

~Robert Louis Stevenson

What if

vulnerability

is a position

of strength?

Your pain is the breaking of the shell
that encloses your understanding.

~Kahlil Gibran

What if

pain is

resistance

to feeling?

If you are pained by external things, it is not they that disturb you, but your own judgment of them. And it is in your power to wipe out that judgment now.

~Marcus Aurelius

judgment

causes pain?

A man's first care should be to avoid
the reproaches of his own heart.

~Joseph Addison

any judgment is

self-judgment?

The meeting of two personalities
is like the contact of two chemical
substances. If there is any reaction,
both are transformed.

~Carl Gustav Jung

What if

resentments

dissolve as

judgment is

transformed?

People are not disturbed by things,
but by the view they take of them.

~*Epictetus*

What if

you are

totally safe?

Every artist drips his brush in
his own soul, and paints his own
nature into his pictures.

~Henry Ward Beecher

What if

whatever occurs

in your life is for

your benefit?

We are all born for love. It is the principle of existence, and its only end.

~Benjamin Disraeli

life is love's

longing to

know itself?

The world is a looking glass
and gives back to every man the
reflection of his own face.

~William M. Thackeray

What if

life acts as

a mirror?

When the soul wishes to experience
something she throws an image
of the experience out before her
and enters into her own image.

~Meister Eckhart

What if

daily existence

reflects your

beliefs?

We are slow to believe what if believed
would hurt our feelings.

~Ovid

What if

your beliefs

generate

the emotions

you feel?

Here the heart
May give a useful lesson to the head.

~William Cowper

What if

emotions

vibrate the

intellect beyond

comfortable

concepts?

Curving back within myself
I create again and again.

~Bhagavad Gita

What if

emotions thrust

thoughts into

physical

manifestation?

"I have done that," says my memory.
"I cannot have done that"—says
my pride, and remains adamant.
At last—memory yields.

~Friedrich Nietzsche

emotions

activate

memory?

Men willingly believe what they wish.

~Julius Caesar

What if

memory is

selective?

The more responsible you are in directing your conscious mind with positive thoughts from the heart, the more your spirit can speed up the process of learning and growing, and you can move on into a more fulfilling life. Without the heart perspective, the unmanaged head will keep re-creating the same old negative thoughts and feelings from the unconscious cellular programs in your memory.

~Sara Paddison

What if

your beliefs

structure

what you

remember?

There are two ways to be fooled.
One is to believe what isn't true; the
other is to refuse to believe what is true.

~*Søren Kierkegaard*

What if

beliefs are

information

collectors?

There is nothing covered that
shall not be revealed; neither hid,
that shall not be known.

~Luke 12:2

What if

facts are

invisible beliefs?

We can believe what we choose.

~John Henry Newman

What if

beliefs can be

outgrown?

Whenever you find that a belief limits
your openness, you're free to let it go.

~Raphael Cushnir

What if

you can change

your life by

updating your

beliefs?

The Possible's slow fuse
is lit by the Imagination.

~Emily Dickinson

imagination

presents options?

The present moment is the
only moment available to us,
and it is the door to all moments.

~*Thích Nh'ât Hahn*

What if

now is the

decisive

moment?

One who lives in the present
lives in eternity.

~Ludwig Wittgenstein

What if

this moment is

one of infinite

potential?

If you believe that feeling bad or worrying long enough will change a past or future event, then you are residing on another planet with a different reality system.

~William James

What if

projecting fear

into the future

produces worry?

When we choose to keep the past
more alive than the present, we interfere
with the flow of the life force.

~Caroline Myss

living in the

past creates

blockages now?

The moment your attention
turns to the Now, you feel a
presence, a stillness, a peace.

~Eckhart Tolle

being in

the present

moment fosters

inner peace?

When you find the peace within yourself, you become the kind of person who can live at peace with others.

~Peace Pilgram

inner peace leads

to kindness?

Kindness in words creates confidence.
Kindness in thinking creates profundity.
Kindness in giving creates love.

~Lao-Tsu

kindness

contributes to

harmony?

Do we love enough to change the cycles
of polarity, rising above the judgment
of light and dark to a place where all
experience is viewed as creation
knowing itself, experiencing the
consequences of its own choice.

~Gregg Braden

all paths

are valid?

You are the only master.
Who else?
Subdue yourself,
And discover your master.

~Buddha

What if

you are your

own best

teacher?

Listen and attend with
the ear of your heart.

~St. Benedict

gentle lessons

surround you?

Life is a succession of lessons which
must be lived to be understood.

~Helen Keller

What if

lessons are

to help you

remember

who you are?

Our greatest glory is not in never falling,
but in rising every time we fall.

~*Confucius*

What if

lessons become

more challenging

to get your

attention?

When we allow ourselves quiet
and inner contact regularly, we no
longer need to get sick in order for
our inner self to get our attention.

~Shakti Gawain

suppressed

emotions

generate

dis-ease?

A bodily disease, which we look upon as whole and entire within itself, may, after all, be but a symptom of some ailment in the spiritual part.

~Nathaniel Hawthorne

disease within

the body is

a reflection

of dis-ease

emotionally?

Healing may not be so much about
getting better, as about letting go
of everything that isn't you—all of
the expectations, all of the beliefs—
and becoming who you are.

~Rachael Naomi Remen

judgment stands

between dis-ease

and wellness?

Natural forces within us are
the true healers of disease.

~Hippocrates

What if

by embracing

all facets of

yourself you

can be well?

Love is the great miracle cure. Loving
ourselves works miracles in our lives.

~Louise L. Hay

feeling love

enhances you

physiologically?

Love is everything. It is the key
to life, and its influences are those
that move the world.

~Ralph Waldo Trine

love is the

language

of life?

It's never too late to be what
you might have been.

~George Eliot

What if

what you believe

about yourself

will manifest?

By recognizing that we can see
ourselves in others, every relationship
becomes a tool for the evolution
of our consciousness.

~Deepak Chopra

every

self-affirmation

helps others too?

Do not anticipate trouble, or
worry about what may never happen.
Keep in the sunlight.

~Benjamin Franklin

What if

what you

intend creates

what you

experience?

Intentions are the energy of your
soul coming into contact with
your physical reality.

~Wayne Dyer

What if

intentions

produce

different

outcomes

than wishes?

As you are focusing on 'have not,'
you are not focusing on 'have.'
Whatever you put your focus or energy
into is what you will draw to you.

~Jani King

What if

you empower

what you

focus upon?

Intuition is a gift from the Universe—
from God, if you will—that will
guide us unerringly to the realization
of our hopes and dreams.

~Lynn A. Robinson

What if

intuition

provides

guidance

from the

inner self?

One of the most interesting things about
apparently synchronistic events is that
they change apparently unrelated,
meaningless events into importantly
meaningful ones; they illuminate
the humdrum aspects of life.

~Charles T. Tart

synchronicities

offer

confirmation?

I've dreamt in my life dreams that have
stayed with me ever after, and changed
my ideas; they've gone through and
through me, like wine through water,
and altered the color of my mind.

~Emily Brontë

dreams present

creative insights?

The fundamental nature of spirit
is creation; creativity is its
human counterpart.

~Tobin Hart

What if

creativity is love

expressing itself?

The essence of all beauty, I call love.

~Elizabeth Barrett Browning

beauty awakens

the inner self?

There is no method.
There is only attention, observation.

~Jiddu Krishnamurti

looking within

is about attitude,

not technique?

You *can* produce a State of Being by simply *selecting one*. And you can do this *anytime, anywhere*.

~Neale Donald Walsch

What if

attitude

determines

perspective?

We choose what attitudes we have right now. And it's a continuing choice.

~John Maxwell

What if

new options

present

themselves

as attitudes

change?

Do all the good you can,
By all the means you can,
In all the ways you can,
In all the places you can,
At all the times you can,
To all the people you can,
As long as ever you can.

~John Wesley

What if

one loving

thought can

shift the pattern

of your life?

One word frees us of all the weight and
pain of life: That word is love.

~*Sophocles*

What if

every single time

you choose love

you are changing

your reality?

This is the miracle that happens
every time to those who really love;—
the more they give,
the more they possess.

~Rainer Maria Rilke

the more you

choose love, the

more love flows

into your life?

Love and Joy are twins,
or born of each other.

~William Hazlitt

What if

joy arises as

you live in the

flow of love?

The One is none other than the All,
the All none other than the One.

~Seng Ts'an

you are

not alone?

We are the leaves of one branch,
the drops of one sea,
the flowers of one garden.

~Jean-Baptiste Henry Lacordaire

What if

separation is

an illusion?

Humankind has not woven the web of
life. We are but one thread within it.
Whatever we do to the web,
we do to ourselves. All things are
bound together. All things connect.

~Chief Seattle

all is

interconnected?

The same stream of life that runs
through my veins night and day,
runs through the world and
dances in rhythmic measure.

~Radindranath Tagore

you contain all

the information

of the whole?

Invisible quantum waves are spreading
out from each of us and permeating
into all other organisms.

~Mae Wan Ho

you broadcast a

frequency that

others receive?

Creative or loving or caring thoughts
invoke high-frequency emotions, such as
appreciation, forgiveness and joy, and
raise the frequency of your system.

~Gary Zukav

What if

your frequency

expands as you

emanate love?

In this interconnected universe, every improvement we make in our private world improves the world at large for everyone.

~David Hawkins

What if

expanding your

awareness

benefits all

that exists?

We look forward to the time when
the Power of Love will replace the
Love of Power. Then will our world
know the blessings of peace.

~William Ewart Gladstone

love is the

most powerful

force there is?

Love in its essence is spiritual fire.

~Emanuel Swedenborg

you are a

being of love?

Each of us inevitable; Each of us limitless; Each of us with his or her right upon the earth; Each of us allowed the eternal purports of the earth; Each of us here as divinely as any is here.

~Walt Whitman

your potential

is limitless?

Our natural state of being is a relationship—a tango—a constant state of one influencing the other.

~Lynne McTaggart

What if

who you

are changes

the world?

The realization of the self is only
possible if one is productive, if one can
give birth to one's own potentialities.

~*Johann Wolfgang von Goethe*

THE RESOURCES

Bibliography & Resources

Body Awareness/Wellness

Anderson, Greg. *The 22 Non-Negotiable Laws of Wellness: Take Your Health into Your Own Hands to Feel, Think, and Live Better Than You Ever Thought Possible.* New York: HarperSanFrancisco, 1995.

Avila, Elena, and Joy Parker. *Woman Who Glows in the Dark: A Curandera Reveals Traditional Aztec Secrets of Physical and Spiritual Health.* Los Angeles: Jeremy P. Tarcher, 2000.

Ballentine, Rudolph. *Radical Healing: Mind-Body Medicine at its Most Practical and Transformative.* London: Rider, 1999.

Bishop, Ross. *Healing the Shadow.* Santa Fe, NM: Blue Lotus Press, 1998.

Borysenko, Joan. *Minding the Body, Mending the Mind.* Redding, MA: Addison-Wesley, 1987.

Borysenko, Joan, and Myroslav Borysenko. *The Power of the Mind to Heal.* Carson, CA: Hay House, 1994.

Brennan, Barbara Ann. *Hands of Light: A Guide to Healing Through the Human Energy Field.* New York: Bantam, 1987.

___. *Light Emerging: The Journey of Personal Healing.* New York: Bantam, 1993.

Breyere, Rosalyn L. *Wheels of Light: A Study of the Chakras.* Arcadia, CA: Bon Productions, 1989.

Brugh, Joy W. *Joy's Way: A Map for the Transformational Journey: An Introduction to the Potentials for Healing.* New York: Penguin Putnam, 1979.

Bush, Carol A. *Healing Imagery and Music*. Portland, OR: Rudra Press, 1995.

Campbell, Don. *The Mozart Effect: Tapping the Power of Music to Heal the Body, Strengthen the Mind, and Unlock the Creative Spirit*. New York: Quill, 2001.

Childre, Doc. *Freeze-Frame: One Minute Stress Management: A Scientifically Proven Technique for Clear Decision Making and Improved Health*. Boulder Creek, CA: Planetary Publications, 1998.

Chopra, Deepak. *Ageless Body, Timeless Mind: The Quantum Alternative to Growing Old*. New York: Harmony Books, 1993.

___. *The Path to Love: Spiritual Strategies for Healing*. New York: Three Rivers Press, 1998.

___. *Quantum Healing: Exploring the Frontiers of Mind/Body Medicine*. New York: Bantam Books, 1989.

Cousins, Norman. *Head First: The Biology of Hope and the Healing Power of the Human Spirit*. New York: Penguin, 1990.

Davies, Brenda. *The 7 Healing Chakras: Unlocking Your Body's Energy Centers*. Berkeley, CA: Ulysses Press, 2000.

Dethlefsen, Thorwalk, and Rüdiger Dahlke. *The Healing Power of Illness: Understanding What Your Symptoms Are Telling You*. New York: Sterling, 2002.

Diamond, John. *Life Energy: Using the Meridians to Unlock the Hidden Power of Your Emotions*. St Paul, MN: Paragon House, 1998.

___. *Your Body Doesn't Lie: Unlock the Power of Your Natural Energy!* New York: Warner Books, 1994.

Dossey, Larry. *Healing Words: The Power of Prayer and the Practice of Medicine*. San Francisco: HarperSan Francisco, 1993.

___. *Prayer Is Good Medicine: How to Reap the Healing Benefits of Prayer.* San Francisco: HarperSan Francisco, 1996.

___. *Reinventing Medicine: Beyond Mind-Body to a New Era of Healing.* San Francisco: HarperSan Francisco, 1999.

Dziemidko, Helen E. *The Complete Book of Energy Medicines: Choosing Your Path to Health.* Rochester, VT: Inner Traditions, 1999.

Eden, Donna, and David Feinstein. *Energy Medicine.* New York: Jeremy P. Tarcher-Putnam, 1998.

Emery, Marcia. *The Intuitive Healer: Accessing Your Inner Physician.* New York: St. Martin's Griffin, 2000.

Epstein, Gerald. *Healing Visualizations: Creating Health Through Imagery.* New York: Bantam Books, 1989.

Epstein, Mark. *Going to Pieces Without Falling Apart: A Buddhist Perspective on Wholeness.* New York: Broadway Books, 1999.

Farhi, Donna. *The Breathing Book: Good Health and Vitality Through Essential Breath Work.* New York: Henry Holt & Co., 1996.

Gabbay, Simone. *Visionary Medicine: Real Hope for Total Healing.* Virginia Beach, VA: A.R.E. Press, 2003.

Gawain, Shakti. *The Path of Transformation: How Healing Ourselves Can Change the World.* Novato, CA: New World Library, 2000.

Gendlin, Eugene T. *Let Your Body Interpret Your Dreams.* Williamette, Illinois: Chiron Publications, 1986.

Gerber, Richard. *A Practical Guide to Vibrational Medicine: Energy Healing and Spiritual Transformation.* New York: Quill, 2001.

___. *Vibrational Medicine: The #1 Handbook of Subtle-Energy Therapies.* Rochester, VT: Inner Traditions, 2001.

Goldman, Jonathan. *Healing Sounds: The Power of Harmonics*. Rochester, VT: Inner Traditions, 2002.

Goldsmith, Joel S. *The Art of Spiritual Healing*. New York: HarperCollins, 1992.

Goleman, Daniel, ed. *Healing Emotions: Conversations With the Dalai Lama on Mindfulness, Emotions, and Health*. Boston: Shambhala, 2003.

Gordon, Richard. *Quantum-Touch: The Power to Heal*. Berkeley, CA: North Atlantic Books, 2002.

Graham, Helen. *Soul Medicine: Restoring the Spirit to Healing*. London: Newleaf, 2001.

Griscom, Chris. *The Healing of Emotion: Awakening the Fearless Self*. Galisteo, NM: Light Institute Press, 1990.

Hartley, Linda. *Wisdom of the Body Moving: An Introduction to Body-Mind Centering*. Berkeley, CA: North Atlantic Books, 1995.

Hay, Louise L. *Heal Your Body: The Mental Causes for Physical Illness and the Metaphysical Way to Overcome Them*. Carlsbad, CA: Hay House, 1994.

___. *You Can Heal Your Life*. Carlsbad, CA: Hay House, 1999.

Heller, Joseph, and William A. Henkin. *Bodywise*. Oakland, CA: Wingbow Press, 1991.

Jahnke, Roger. *The Healing Promise of Qi: Creating Extraordinary Wellness Through Qigong and Tai Chi*. New York: McGraw-Hill Contemporary Books, 2002.

Johari, Harish. *Chakras: Energy Centers of Transformation*. Rochester, VT: Inner Traditions, 2000.

Judith, Anodea. *Wheels of Life: A User's Guide to the Chakra System*. St. Paul, MN: Llewellyn Publications, 2002.

Kabat-Zinn Jon. *Full Catastrophe Living: Using the Wisdom of Your Body and Mind to Face Stress, Pain, and Illness*. New York: Delta, 1990.

Kelder, Peter. *Ancient Secret of the Fountain of Youth*. New York: Doubleday, 1998.

Klein, Bob. *Movements of Magic: The Spirit of Tai-Chi-Chuan*. New York: HarperCollins, 1987.

Krieger, Delores. *Accepting Your Power to Heal*. Santa Fe: Bear & Co., 1993.

___. *The Therapeutic Touch: How to Use Your Hands to Help or Heal*. New York: Prentice-Hall, 1986.

Kurzweil, Ray, with Terry Grossman. *Fantastic Voyage: Live Long Enough to Live Forever*. New York: Rodale, 2004.

Lamb, F. Bruce. *Rio Tigre and Beyond*. Berkeley, CA: North Atlantic Books, 1985.

Leadbetter, C. W. *The Chakras*. Wheaton, IL: Theosophical Publishing House, 1974.

Liberman, Jacob. *Light: Medicine of the Future*. Santa Fe: Bear & Co., 1991.

Lingerman, Hal A. *The Healing Energies of Music*. Wheaton, IL: Theosophical Publishing House, 1983.

Liu, Hong, and Paul Perry. *The Healing Art of Qi Gong: Ancient Wisdom from a Modern Master*. New York: Warner Books, 1999.

Mason, Keith. *Medicine for the Twenty-First Century: The Key to Healing with Vibrational Medicine*. Shaftesbury, Dorset: Element, 1992.

Masters, Robert. *Neurospeak: Transforms Your Body, While You Read.* Wheaton, IL: Quest Books-The Theosophical Publishing House, 1994.

Masters, Roy. *How Your Mind Can Keep You Well*. Los Angeles: Foundation Books, 1972.

Matthews, Dave A. *The Faith Factor: Proof of the Healing Power of Prayer*. New York: Viking, 1998.

McGarey, William A. *In Search of Healing: Whole-Body-Healing through Mind-Body-Spirit Connection*. New York: Perigree, 1996.

Mehl-Madrona, Lewis. *Coyote Medicine: Lessons From Native American Healing*. New York: Fireside, 1998.

Mendoza, Maya. *The Hidden Power of Emotional Intuition: Use the Healing Power of Your Mind to Promote Health & Happiness*. New York: Vega, 2003.

Moondance, Wolf. *Star Medicine: Native American Path to Emotional Healing*. New York: Sterling, 1997.

Moyers, Bill. *Healing and the Mind*. New York: Doubleday, 1993.

Myss, Caroline. *Anatomy of the Spirit: The Seven Stages of Power and Healing*. New York: Three Rivers Press, 1996.

___. *Why People Don't Heal and How They Can*. New York: Three Rivers Press, 1998.

Myss, Caroline, and C. Norman Shealy. *The Creation of Health: The Emotional, Psychological, and Spiritual Responses That Promote Health and Healing*. New York: Three Rivers Press, 1998.

Northrup, Christiane. *Women's Bodies, Women's Wisdom*. New York: Bantam, 2002.

Olson, Stuart Alve. *Tao of No Stress: Three Simple Paths*. Rochester, VT: Inner Traditions, 2002.

Orloff, Judith. *Dr. Judith Orloff's Guide to Intuitive Healing: Five Steps to Physical, Emotional, and Sexual Wellness*. New York: Three Rivers Press, 2001.

___. *Positive Energy: 10 Extraordinary Prescriptions for Transforming Fatigue, Stress, and Fear into Vibrance, Strength and Love*. New York: Harmony, 2004.

Paulsen, Genevieve Lewis. *Kundalini and the Chakras: A Practical Manual-Evolution in This Lifetime*. St. Paul, MN: Llewellyn, 2002.

Pearsall, Paul. *The Beethoven Factor: The New Positive Psychology of Hardiness, Happiness, Healing and Hope*. Charlottesville, VA: Hampton Roads, 2003.

___. *The Heart's Code: Tapping the Wisdom and Power of Our Heart Energy: The New Findings About Cellular Memories and Their Role in the Mind/Body/Spirit Connection*. New York: Broadway Books, 1999.

Pert, Candace B. *Molecules Of Emotion: The Science Behind Mind-Body Medicine*. New York: Simon & Schuster, 1999.

Ramacharaka, Yogi. *Science of Breath: A Complete Manual of the Oriental Breathing Philosophy*. Chicago: Yogi Publication Society, 1904.

Reed, Henry, and Brenda English. *The Intuitive Heart. How to Trust Your Intuition for Guidance and Healing*. Virginia Beach, VA: A.R.E. Press, 2000.

Rush, Martin. *Decoding the Secret Language of Your Body: The Many Ways Our Bodies Send Us Messages*. New York: Fireside, 1994.

Schiffmann, Erich. *Yoga The Spirit And Practice Of Moving Into Stillness*. New York: Pocket Books, 1996.

Schulz, Mona Lisa. *Awakening Intuition: Using Your Mind-Body Network for Insight and Healing*. New York: Three Rivers Press, 1999.

Schwarz, Jack. *Voluntary Controls: Exercises for Creative Meditation and for Activating the Potential of the Chakras*. New York: Dutton, 1978.

Scott-Mumby, Keith. *Virtual Medicine: A New Dimension in Energy Healing*. London: Thorsons, 1999.

Shapiro, Debbie. *The Body Mind Workbook: Explaining How the Mind and Body Work Together*. New York: Sterling, 2002.

Shealy, C. Norman. *Sacred Healing: The Curing Power of Energy and Spirituality*. Boston: Element, 1999.

Sherwood, Keith. *Chakra Therapy: For Personal Growth and Healing*. St. Paul, MN: Llewellyn Publications, 1988.

Siegel, Bernie S. *Love, Medicine, and Miracles: Lessons Learned about Self-Healing from a Surgeon's Experience with Exceptional Patients*. New York: Harper Perennial, 1998.

___. *Peace, Love and Healing: Bodymind Communication & the Path to Self-Healing: An Exploration.* New York: Harper Perennial, 1998.

Sutherland, Caroline M. *The Body "Knows": How to Tune In to Your Body and Improve Your Health.* Carlsbad, CA: Hay House, 2001.

Tame, David. *The Secret Power of Music: The Transformation of Self and Society Through Musical Energy.* New York: Destiny, 1984.

Tick, Edward. *The Practice of Dream Healing.* Wheaton, IL: Quest, 2001.

Villoldo, Alberto. *Shaman, Healer, Sage: How to Heal Yourself and Others with the Energy Medicine of the Americas.* New York: Harmony, 2000.

Virtue, Doreen. *Chakra Clearing.* Carlsbad, CA: Hay House, 1998.

Weil, Andrew. *Health and Healing: Understanding Conventional and Alternative Medicine.* Boston: Houghton Mifflin, 1998.

___. *Natural Health, Natural Medicine.* Boston: Houghton Mifflin, 1998.

___. *Spontaneous Healing: How to Discover and Embrace Your Body's Natural Ability to Maintain and Heal Itself.* New York: Ballantine Books, 2000.

Weiss, Brian. *Mirrors of Time: Using Regression for Physical, Emotional, and Spiritual Healing.* Carlsbad, CA: Hay House, 2002.

___. *Through Time into Healing.* New York: Simon & Schuster, 1992.

Children/Education/Parenting

Aron, Elaine N. *The Highly Sensitive Child: Helping Our Children Thrive When the World Overwhelms Them.* New York: Broadway, 2002.

Asher, James J. *Brainswitching: A Skill For the 21st Century.* Los Gatos, CA: Sky Oaks Productions, 1988.

Atkins, Dale. *I'm OK, You're My Parents: How to Overcome Guilt, Let Go of Anger, and Create a Relationship That Works.* New York: Henry Holt, 2004.

Atwater, P.M.H. *The New Children and Near Death Experiences.* Rochester, VT: Inner Traditions, 2003.

Bailey, Joseph. *Slowing Down to the Speed of Love: How to Create a Deeper, More Fulfilling Relationship in a Hurried World.* New York: McGraw-Hill, 2003.

Berenda, Polly Berrien. *Gently Lead: How to Teach Your Children about God While Finding Out for Yourself.* New York: Harper Collins, 1991.

Bowman, Carol. *Children's Past Lives: How Past Life Memories Affect Your Child.* New York: Bantam Books, 1997.

Burmyn, Lynne, and Christina Baldwin. *Sun Signs for Kids: An Astrological Guide For Parents.* New York: St. Martin's Press, 1985.

Burns, Litany. *The Sixth Sense of Children.* New York: New American Library, 2002.

Buzan, Tony. *Mind Maps for Kids: The Shortcut to Success at School.* New York: HarperCollins, 2003.

Campbell, Don. *The Mozart Effect for Children: Awakening Your Child's Mind, Health, and Creativity with Music.* New York: Quill, 2002.

Carroll, Lee, and Jan Tober. *The Indigo Children: The New Children Have Arrived.* Carlsbad, CA: Hay House, 1999.

Carter, Forrest. *The Education of Little Tree.* Albuquerque: University of New Mexico Press, 1976.

Chamberlain, David B. *The Mind of Your Newborn Baby.* Berkeley, CA: North Atlantic Books, 1998.

Childre, Doc. *The How to Book of Teen Self Discovery: Helping Teens Find Balance, Security and Esteem.* Boulder Creek, CA: Planetary Publications, 1994.

Choquette, Sonia. *The Wise Child: A Spiritual Guide to Nurturing Your Child's Intuition.* New York: Three Rivers Press, 1999.

Covey, Stephen, R. *The Seven Habits of Highly Effective Families: Building a Beautiful Family Culture in a Turbulent World.* New York: Golden Books, 1997.

Dancy, Rahima Baldwin. *You Are Your Child's 1st Teacher.* Berkeley, CA: Celestial Arts, 2000.

Day, Peggy Rose, and Susan Gale. *Edgar Cayce on the Indigo Children.* Virginia Beach, VA: A.R.E. Press, 2004.

Dennis, Caryl, and Parker Whitman. *The Millennium Children: Tales of the Shift.* Clearwater, FL: Rainbows Unlimited, 1997.

Dennison, Paul E., and Gail E. Dennison. *Brain Gym: Simple Activities for Whole Brain Learning.* Ventura, CA: Edu-Kinesthetics, 1986.

DePorter, Bobbi, Mark Reardon, and Sarah Singer-Nourie. *Quantum Teaching: Orchestrating Student Success.* Needham Heights, MA: Pearson, Allyn and Bacon, 1998.

Doe, Mimi, and Marsha F. Walch. *10 Principles for Spiritual Parenting: Nurturing Your Child's Soul.* New York: Perennial 1998.

Dryden, Gorden, and Jeannette Vos. *The Learning Revolution: To Change the Way the World Learns*. Torrance, CA: The Learning Web, 1999.

Eisler, Riane. *Tomorrow's Children: A Blueprint for Partnership Education in the 21st Century*. Boulder, CO: Westview Press, 2000.

Elias, Maurice J., Steven E. Tobias and Brian S. Friedlander. *Raising Emotionally Intelligent Teenagers: Guiding the Way for Compassionate, Committed, Courageous Adults*. New York: Three Rivers Press, 2002.

Fitzpatrick, Jean Grasso. *Something More: Nurturing Your Child's Spiritual Growth*. New York: Viking Penguin, 1992.

Gardner, Howard. *Intelligence Reframed: Multiple Intelligences for the 21st Century*. New York: Basic Books, 1999.

Gordon, F. Noah. *Magical Classroom: Creating Effective, Brain-friendly Environments for Learning*. Tucson, AZ: Zephyr Press, 1995.

Groome, Thomas H. *Educating for Life: A Spiritual Vision for Every Teacher and Parent*. New York: Crossroad-Herder & Herder, 2001.

Hallett, Elisabeth. *Soul Trek: Meeting Our Children on the Way to Birth*. Hamilton, Montana: Light Hearts Publishing, 1995.

___. *Stories of the Unborn Soul: The Mystery and Delight of Pre-Birth Communication*. San Jose, CA: The Writers Club Press, 2002.

Hannaford, Carla. *Awakening the Child Heart: Handbook for the Global Parenting*. Captain Cook, HI: Jamilla Nur, 2002.

___. *Smart Moves: Why Learning is Not All In Your Head*. Arlington, VA: Great Ocean Publishers, 1995.

Harrison, Steven. *The Happy Child: Changing the Heart of Education*. Boulder, CO: Sentient Publications, 2002.

Hart, Tobin. *From Information to Transformation: Education for the Evolution of Consciousness.* New York: Peter Lang Publishing, 2001.

___. *The Secret Spiritual World of Children: The Breatkthrough Discovery That Profoundly Alters Our Conventional View of Children's Mystical Experiences.* Makawao, HI: Inner Ocean Publishing, 2003.

Hirsh-Pasek, Kathy, and Roberta Michnick Golinkoff, with Diane Eyer. *Einstein Never Used Flash Cards: How Our Children REALLY Learn—and Why They Need to Play More and Memorize Less.* Emmaus, PA: Rodale, 2003.

Hoffman, Edward. *Visions of Innocence: Spiritual and Inspirational Experiences of Childhood.* Boston: Shambhala, 1992.

Hollander, Annette. *How to Help Your Child Have a Spiritual Life: A Parent's Guide to Inner Development.* New York: A & W Publishers, Inc., 1980.

Huber, Cheri. *Time-Out…For Parents: A Compassionate Approach to Parenting.* Murphys, CA: Keep It Simple Books, 1994.

Jampolsky, Gerald, and Lee Jampolsky. *Listen to Me: A Book for Women and Men About Father-Son Relationships.* Berkeley, CA: Celestial Arts, 1996.

Jenkins, Peggy J. *Nurturing Spirituality in Children: Simple Hands-On Activities.* Hillsboro, OR: Beyond Worlds Publishing, Inc., 1995.

Kabat-Zinn, Myla, and Jon Kabat-Zinn. *Everyday Blessing: The Inner Work of Mindful Parenting.* New York: Hyperion 1998.

Kessler, Rachel. *The Soul of Education: Helping Students Find Connection, Compassion, and Character at School.* Alexandria, VA: Association for Supervision & Curriculum Development, 2000.

Kline, Peter. *The Everyday Genius: Restoring Children's Natural Joy of Learning, and Yours Too*. Arlington, VA: Great Ocean Publishers, 1997.

Krishnamurti, Jiddu. *Krishnamurti on Education*, ed. Krishnamurti Foundation Trust Limited. New York: Harper & Row, 1974.

Kurcinka, Mary Sheedy. *Raising Your Spirited Child: A Guide for Parents Whose Child Is More Intense, Sensitive, Perceptive, Persistent, Energetic*. New York: Perennial, 1998.

Lantieri, Linda, ed. *Schools With Spirit: Nurturing the Inner Lives of Children and Teachers*. Boston: Beacon Press, 2001.

Loomans, Diane, with Julia Loomans. *Full Esteem Ahead: 100 Ways to Build Self-Esteem in Children and Adults*. Tuburton, CA: Kramer, 1994.

Maiden, Anne H., and Edie Farwell. *The Tibetan Art of Parenting*. Boston, MA: Wisdom Publications, 1997.

Maruilies, Nancy. *Mapping Inner Space: Learning and Teaching Visual Mapping*. Tucson: Zephyr Press, 2001.

McGraw, Phil. *Family First: Your Step-by-Step Plan for Creating a Phenomenal Family*. New York: Free Press, 2004.

Medhus, Eliza. *Raising Children Who Think for Themselves*. Hillsboro, OR: Beyond Words Publishing, 2001.

Miller, John P. *Education and the Soul: Towards a Spiritual Curriculum*. Albany, NY: State University of New York Press, 1999.

Montessori, Maria. *The Absorbent Mind*. New York: Henry Holt & Co., 1995.

Nadham, Gary Paul, and Stephen Trimble. *Geography of Childhood: Why Children Need Wild Places*. Boston: Beacon Press, 1994.

Olszewski-Kubilias, Lisa Limburg-Weber, and Steven Pfeiffer. *Early Gifts: Recognizing and Nurturing Children's Talents*. Waco, TX: Prufrock Press, 2003.

Pearce, Joseph Chilton. *From Magical Child to Magical Teen: A Guide to Adolescent Development*. Rochester, VT: Inner Traditions, 2003.

___. *Magical Child: Rediscovering Nature's Plan for Our Children*. New York: Bantam Books, 1981.

Powell, Tag, and Carol Howell Mills. *ESP for Kids: How to Develop Your Child's Psychic Ability*. Key Largo: Top of the Mountain Publishing, 1993.

Prashnig, Barbara. *The Power of Diversity: New Ways of Learning and Teaching*. Auckland, New Zealand: David Bateman, 1998.

Prather, Hugh, and Gayle Prather. *Spiritual Parenting: A Guide to Understanding and Nurturing the Heart of Your Child*. New York: Harmony Books, 1996.

Rain, Mary Summer. *Mountains, Meadows and Moonbeams: A Child's Spiritual Reader*. Charlottesville, VA: Hampton Roads, 1992.

Restak, Richard M. *The Infant Mind*. New York: Doubleday, 1986.

Rosenberg, Marshall B. *Life-Enriching Education: Nonviolent Communication Helps Schools Improve Performance, Reduce Conflict, and Enhance Relationships*. Encinitas, CA: PuddleDancer Press, 2003.

Rozman, Deborah. *Meditating with Children: The Art of Concentration and Centering*. Boulder Creek, CA: Planetary Publications, 1994.

Silverman, Linda Kreger. *Upside Down Brilliance: The Visual-Spatial Learner*. Denver, CO: DeLeon Publishing, 2002.

Singer, Dorothy G., and Jerome L. Singer. *The House of Make-Believe: Children's Play and the Developing Imagination*. Cambridge, MA: Harvard University Press, 1992.

Sinetar, Marsha. *Spiritual Intelligence: What We Can Learn from the Early Awakening Child*. Maryknoll, NY: Orbis Books, 2000.

Smith, Michael. *Questions for Kids: A Book to Discover a Child's Imagination and Knowledge*. Gardena CA: East West Discovery Press, 2003.

Spangler, David. *Parent As Mystic, Mystic As Parent*. New York: Riverhead, 2000.

Stevenson, Ian. *Children Who Remember Previous Lives: A Question of Reincarnation*. Charlottesville, VA: University Press of Virginia. 1987.

Tagore, Rabindranath, *Rabindranath Tagore: Pioneer in Education*. London: John Murray, 1961.

Tapscott, Don. *Growing Up Digital: The Rise of the Net Generation*. New York: McGraw Hill, 1998.

Van Praagh, James. *Looking Beyond: A Teen's Guide to the Spiritual World*. New York: Fireside, 2003.

Verny, Thomas, and John Kelly. *The Secret Life of the Unborn Child*, New York, NY: Dell Publishing, 1981.

Virtue, Doreen. *The Care and Feeding of Indigo Children*. Carlsbad, CA: Hay House, 2001.

___. *The Crystal Children: A Guide to the Newest Generation of Psychic and Sensitive Children*. Carlsbad, CA: Hay House, 2003.

Vitale, Barbara Meister. *Unicorns Are Real: A Right-Brained Approach to Learning*. Torrance, CA: Jalmar Press, 1982.

Youngs, Bettie B. *The 6 Vital Ingredients Of Self-Esteem: How To Develop Them In Your Students*. Torrance, CA: Jalmar Press, 1992.

Personal Growth/Spirituality

Alverga, Alex Polari de. *Forest of Visions: Ayahuasca, Amazonian Spirituality, and the Santo Daime Tradition.* Rochester, VT: Park Street Press, 1999.

Abbott, Edwin A. *Flatland: A Romance of Many Dimensions.* Mineola, NY: Dover, 1992.

Adrienne, Carol. *Find Your Purpose, Change Your Life: Getting to the Heart of Your Life's Mission.* New York: Quill, 2001.

___. *The Purpose of Your Life: Finding Your Place In The World Using Synchronicity, Intuition, And Uncommon Sense.* New York: William Morrow, 1999.

Andreas, Connirae, and Steve Andreas. *Heart of the Mind: Engaging Your Inner Power to Change.* Moab, UT: Real People Press, 1989.

Andrews, Ted. *Animal-Speak: The Spiritual & Magical Powers of Creatures Great & Small.* St. Paul, MN: Llewellyn, 1993.

Atwater, P.M.H. *Future Memory.* Charlottesville, VA: Hampton Roads, 1999.

Auerbach, Loyd. *Mind Over Matter: A Comprehensive Guide to Discovering Your Psychic Powers.* New York: Kensington, 1996.

Bach, Richard. *Illusions: The Adventures of a Reluctant Messiah.* New York: Arrow-Random House, 2001.

___. *There's No Such Place As Far Away.* New York: Delta, 1998.

Bair, Puran. *Living from the Heart: Heart Rhythm Meditation for Energy, Clarity, Peace, Joy, and Inner Power.* New York: Three Rivers Press, 1998.

Ball, Marshall Stewart. *Kiss of God—The Wisdom of a Silent Child*. Deerfield Beach, FL: Health Communications, 1999.

Ban Breathnach, Sarah. *Simple Abundance*. New York: Warner Books, 1995.

___. *Something More: Excavating Your Authentic Self*. New York: Warner Books, 2000.

Baumann, T. Lee. *God at the Speed of Light*. Virginia Beach, VA: A.R.E. Press, 2002.

Beattie, Melody. *Gratitude: Affirming the Good Things in Life*. New York: Hazelden/Ballantine Books, 1992.

Beck, Martha Nibley. *Finding Your Own North Star: Claiming the Life You Were Meant to Live*. New York: Three Rivers Press, 2002.

Bell, Craig S. *Comprehending Coincidence: Synchronicity and Personal Transformation*. Westchester, PA: Chryalis, 2000.

Bennett-Goleman, Tara. *Emotional Alchemy: How the Mind Can Heal the Heart*. New York: Three Rivers Press, 2002.

Bentov, Itzhak. *A Brief Tour of Higher Consciousness: A Cosmic Book on the Mechanics of Creation*. Rochester, VT: Destiny Books, 2000.

___. *Stalking the Wild Pendulum: On the Mechanics of Consciousness*. Rochester, VT: Inner Traditions, 1988.

Besant, Annie Wood, and C. W. Leadbeater. *Thought-forms*. Wheaton, IL: Quest, 1969.

Bethards, Betty. *Be Your Own Guru*. Petaluma, CA: Inner Light Foundation, 2003.

___. *The Dream Book: Symbols for Self Understanding*. Petaluma, CA: New Century Publishers, 2002.

Bolen, Jean Shinoda. *The Millionth Circle: How to Change Ourselves and the World: The Meaning and Maintenance of Women's Circles*. Boston, MA: Conari Press, 1999.

Borysenko, Joan A. *Fire In the Soul: A New Psychology of Spiritual Optimism*. New York: Warner Books, 1993.

___. *Inner Peace for Busy People: 52 Simple Strategies for Transforming Your Life*. Carlsbad, CA: Hay House, 2001.

Braden, Gregg. *The God Code: The Secret of Our Past, the Promise of Our Future*. Carlsbad, CA: Hay House, 2004.

___. *The Isaiah Effect: Decoding the Lost Science Of Prayer and Prophecy*. New York: Three Rivers Press, 2000.

___. *Walking Between the Worlds: The Science of Compassion*. Bellevue, WA: Radio Bookstore Press, 1997.

Bragdon, Emma. *The Call of Spiritual Emergency*. New York: Harper & Row, 1990.

Brandon, Nathaniel. *Honoring the Self: Self-Esteem and Personal Tranformation*. New York: Bantam Books, 1985.

Brinkley, Dannion. *At Peace in the Light*. New York: HarperTorch, 1996.

Bucke, Richard Maurice. *Cosmic Consciousness*. New York: Dutton, 1991.

Burnham, Sophy. *A Book of Angels*. New York: Ballantine Books, 1991.

Buscaglia, Leo F. *Love: What Life Is All About*. New York: Ballantine Books, 1996.

Caddy, Eileen. *God Spoke to Me*. Forres, Scotland: The Findhorn Press, 1992.

___. *Opening Door Within*. Forres, Scotland: The Findhorn Press, 1987.

Cameron, Julia. *The Artist's Way: A Spiritual Path to Higher Creativity*. New York: Jeremy P. Tarcher/Putnam, 1992.

___. *Walking in This World: The Practical Art of Creativity*. New York: Jeremy P. Tacher/Putnam, 2002.

Carey, Ken. *Vision: A Personal Call to Create a New World*. San Francisco: Harper SanFrancisco, 1992.

Carpenter, Tom, and Linda Carpenter. *Dialogue on Awakening*. Port Ludlow, WA: Carpenters Press, 2001.

Carse, James. *Finite and Infinite Games: A Vision of Life as Play and Possibility*. New York: Ballantine Books, 1986.

Castaneda, Carlos. *The Fire From Within*. New York: Pocket Books, 1991.

Cayce, Edgar. *Auras: An Essay on the Meaning of Colors*. Virginia Beach, VA: A.R.E. Press, 1989.

Cayce, Hugh Lynn. *Venture Inward: A Guide to the Doorways to Inner Exploration*. Virginia Beach, VA: A.R.E. Press, 1996.

Chinmoy, Sri. *God is…*New York: Aum Publications, 1997.

Chödrön, Pema. *The Places That Scare You: A Guide to Fearlessness in Difficult Times*. Boston: Shambhala, 2001.

___. *When Things Fall Apart: Heart Advice for Difficult Times*. Boston: Shambhala, 1997.

Chopra, Deepak. *How to Know God: The Soul's Journey Into the Mystery of Mysteries*. New York: Three Rivers Press, 2001.

___. *The Spontaneous Fulfillment of Desire: Harnessing the Infinite Power of Coincidence*. New York: Harmony Books, 2003.

Choquette, Sonia. *The Psychic Pathway: A Workbook for Reawakening the Voice of Your Soul*. New York: Three Rivers Press, 1995.

___. *True Balance: A Common Sense Guide for Renewing Your Spirit*. New York: Three Rivers Press, 2000.

Cohen, Alan. *Dragon Doesn't Live Here Anymore: Loving Fully, Living Freely*. New York: Ballantine, 1993.

___. *Wisdom of the Heart: Inspirations for a Life Worth Living*. Carlsbad, CA: Hay House, 2002

Cole-Whittaker, Terry. *What You Think of Me Is None of My Business*. New York: Jove Books, 1998.

Colton, Ann Ree. *Draughts of Remembrance*. Santa Monica, CA: DeVorss & Co., 1959.

Cushnir, Raphael. *Setting Your Heart on Fire: Seven Invitations to Liberate Your Life*. New York: Broadway Books, 2003.

Dass, Ram. *Be Here Now*. San Cristobal, NM: Hanuman Foundation, 1971.

Day, Laura. *The Circle: How the Power of a Single Wish Can Change Your Life*. New York: Jeremy P. Tarcher, 2001.

Doore, Gary. *Shaman's Path: Healing, Personal Growth, and Empowerment*. Boston: Shambhala, 1988.

Dossey, Larry. *Be Careful What You Pray for…You Just Might Get It: What We Can Do About the Unintentional Effect of Our Thoughts, Prayers, and Wishes*. San Francisco: HarperSan Francisco, 1998.

Duncan, Shannon. *Present Moment Awareness*. Novato, CA: New World Library, 2003.

Dwoskin, Hale, and Lester Levenson. *Happiness Is Free: And It's Easier Than You Think!* Sedona, AZ: Sedona Press, 2002.

Dyer, Wayne W. *The Power of Intention: Learning to Co-Create Your World Your Way*. Carlsbad, CA: Hay House, 2004.

___. *10 Secrets for Success and Inner Peace*. Carlsbad, CA: Hay House, 2002.

___. *There's a Spiritual Solution to Every Problem*. New York: Harper-Collins, 2001.

Eadie, Betty J. *Embraced by the Light*. Placerville, CA: Gold Leaf Press, 1992.

Ekman, Paul. *Emotions Revealed: Recognizing Faces and Feelings to Improve Communication and Emotional Life*. New York: Owl Books, 2004.

Einstein, Patricia. *Intuition: The Path to Inner Wisdom—How to Discover and Use Your Greatest Natural Resource*. New York: Sterling, 2002.

Emery, Marcia. *PowerHunch! Living an Intuitive Life*. Hillsboro, OR: Beyond Words Publishing, 2001.

Emoto, Masaru. *The Hidden Messages in Water*. Hillsboro, OR: Beyond Words Publishing, 2004.

Falter-Barnes, Suzanne. *How Much Joy Can You Stand: A Creative Guide to Facing Your Fears and Making Your Dreams Come True*. New York: Ballantine, 2000.

Ferrini, Paul. *Love Without Conditions: Reflections of the Christ Mind*. Greenfield, MA: Heartways Press, 1995.

Feuerstein, Georg. *Lucid Waking: Mindfulness and the Spiritual Potential of Humanity*. Rochester, VT: Inner Traditions, 1997.

Föllmi. Danielle, and Oliver Föllmi: *Offerings: Buddhist Wisdom for Every Day*. New York: Stewart, Tabori & Chang, 2003.

Ford, Debbie. *The Dark Side of the Light Chasers. Reclaiming Your Power, Creativity, Brilliance, and Dreams*. New York: Riverhead, 1999.

___. *The Right Questions: Ten Essential Questions to Guide You to an Extraordinary Life*. New York: HarperCollins, 2003.

Fox, Emmett. *Alter Your Life*. San Francisco: Harper SanFrancisco, 1994.

Frissell, Bob. *You Are a Spiritual Being Having a Human Experience*. Berkeley, CA: Frog Ltd., 2000.

Gawain, Shakti. *Creative Visualization: Use the Power Of Your Imagination to Create What You Want In Your Life*. Novato, CA: New World Library, 2002.

___. *Living in the Light: A Guide to Personal and Planetary Transformation*. Novato, CA: New World Library, 1998.

Gendlin, Eugene T. *Focusing*. New York: Bantam Books, 1988.

Goldsmith, Joel S. *The Infinite Way*, Camarillo, CA: DeVorss & Co, 1979.

___. *Man Was Not Born To Cry*. Atlanta, GA: Acropolis Press, 1998.

Goleman, Daniel. *Emotional Intelligence: Why It Can Matter More Than IQ*. New York: Bantam, 1995.

Grabhorn, Lynn. *Excuse Me, Your Life is Waiting: The Astonishing Power of Feelings*. Charlottesville, VA: Hampton Roads, 2000.

Griscom, Chris. *Psychogenetics: The Force of Heredity*. Galisteo, NM: Light Institute Press, 2000.

Griscom, Chris, Wulfing von Rohr. *Time Is An Illusion*. New York: Fireside, 1986.

Grof, Christina, and Stanislav Grof. *The Stormy Search For The Self: A Guide to Personal Growth Through Transformational Crisis*. Los Angeles: Jeremy P. Tarcher-Perigee Books, 1992.

Grof, Stanislav, and Christina Grof, eds. *Spiritual Emergency: When a Personal Transformation Becomes a Crisis*. Los Angeles: Jeremy P. Tarcher, 1989.

Haich, Elisabeth. *Initiation*. Redway, CA: Seed Center, 1974.

Hall, Manly P. *The Secret Teachings of All Ages*. Los Angeles: Philosophical Research Society, 1994.

Harmon, Willis and Howard Rheingold. *Higher Creativity: Liberating the Unconscious for Breakthrough Insights*. Los Angeles: Jeremy P. Tarcher, 1984.

Harner, Michael. *The Way of the Shaman*. New York: Harper & Row, 1980.

Harrison, Steven. *Doing Nothing: Coming to the End of the Spiritual Search*. Los Angeles: Jeremy P. Tarcher, 1998.

Hart, Mickey. *Drumming at the Edge of Magic*. San Francisco: HarperCollins, 1990.

Hartmann, Thom. *The Last Hours of Ancient Sunlight: Waking Up to Personal and Global Transformation*. New York: Three Rivers Press, 2004.

Hawkins, David R. *The Eye of the I: From Which Nothing is Hidden*. Sedona, AZ: Veritas Publishing, 2001.

___. *I: Reality and Subjectivity*. Sedona, AZ: Veritas Publishing, 2003.

___. *Power vs. Force: An Anatomy of Consciousness: The Hidden Determinants of Human Behavior*. Sedona, AZ: Veritas Publishing, 1995.

Hay, Louise L. *Colors and Numbers: Your Personal Guide to Positive Vibrations in Daily Life*. Carlsbad, CA: Hay House, 2003.

___. *Life*. Carson, CA: Hay House, 1995.

Hendricks, Gay. *Conscious Living: Finding Joy In the Real World*. San Francisco: HarperSan Francisco, 2001.

Hornecker, John. *Cosmic Insights Into Human Expression*. Seattle, WA: Life Sciences Foundation, 1982.

Houston, Jean. *A Mythic Life: Learning to Live Our Greater Story*. New York: HarperCollins, 1996.

___. *The Possible Human : A Course in Enhancing Your Physical, Mental, and Creative Abilities*. Los Angeles: Jeremy P. Tarcher, 1997.

Hubbard, Barbara Marx. *Emergence: The Shift from Ego to Essence*. Charlottesville, VA: Hampton Roads, 2001.

___. *The Revelation: A Message of Hope for the New Millennium*. Novato, CA: Nataraj Publishing, 1995.

Ingram, Catherine. *Passionate Presence: Experiencing the Seven Qualities of Awakened Awareness*. New York: Gotham Books, 2003.

Jaidar, George. *The Soul, an Owner's Manual—Discovering the Fullness of Life*. New York: Paragon House, 1994.

Jampolsky, Gerald G. *Love Is Letting Go Of Fear*. Berkeley, CA: Celestial Arts, 1979.

___. *Shortcuts to God: Finding Peace Quickly Through Practical Spirituality*. Berkeley: Celestial Arts, 2000.

Jung, Carl Gustav. *Memories, Dreams, Reflections*. New York: Vintage Books, 1965.

Jung, Carl Gustav, et al. *Synchronicity: An Acausal Connecting Principle*. Princeton: Princeton Univ. Press, 1973.

Kabat-Zinn, Jon. *Wherever You Go, There You Are*. New York: Hyperion, 1994.

Kalweit, Holger. *Dreamtime and the Inner Space: The World of the Shamans*. Boston: Shambhala, 1988.

Karpinski, Gloria. *Barefoot on Holy Ground: Twelve Lessons in Spiritual Craftsmanship*. New York: Wellspring-Ballantine, 2001.

Katie, Byron, and Stephen Mitchell. *Loving What Is: Four Questions That Can Change Your Life*. New York: Three Rivers Press, 2003.

Keith, Kent M. *Do It Anyway: The Handbook for Finding Personal Meaning and Deep Happiness in a Crazy World*. Makawao, HI: Inner Ocean Publishing, 2003.

King, Jani. *The Gift*. Joshua Tree, CA: Light Source Publishing, 1998.

Kornfield, Jack. *A Path With Heart: A Guide Through the Perils and Promises of Spiritual Life*. New York: Bantam Books, 1993.

Krippner, Stanley. *Human Possibilities*. Garden City, New York: Anchor Press/Doubleday, 1980.

Kübler-Ross, Elisabeth, *On Life After Death*. New York: Celestial Arts, 1991.

Kübler-Ross, Elisabeth, and David Kessler. *Life Lessons: Two Experts on Death and Dying Teach Us About the Mysteries of Life and Living*. New York: Simon & Schuster, 2001.

Larsen, Stephen. *The Shaman's Doorway: Opening the Mythic Imagination to Contemporary Consciousness*. Rochester, VT: Inner Traditions, 1998.

Leonard, George, and Michael Murphy. *The Life We Are Given: A Long-Term Program for Realizing the Potential of Body, Mind, Heart, and Soul.* New York: Jeremy P. Tarcher-Putnam, 1995.

Levitt, Peter. *Fingerpainting on the Moon: Writing and Creativity as a Path to Freedom.* New York: Harmony, 2003.

Lewis, C. S. *Miracles.* New York: Macmillan, 1947.

Lifton, Robert Jay. *The Protean Self: Human Resilience in an Age of Fragmentation.* New York: Basic Books, 1993.

Lundstrom, Meg, and Charlene Belitz. *The Power of Flow: Practical Ways to Transform Your Life With Meaningful Coincidence.* New York: Three Rivers Press, 1998.

Martin, Dianne. *The Book of Intentions.* Hillsboro, OR: Beyond Words Publishing, 2002.

May, Gerald G. *The Dark Night of the Soul: A Psychiatrist Explores the Connection Between Darkness and Spiritual Growth.* San Francisco, Harper SanFrancisco, 2004.

McArthur, Bruce. *Your Life: Why It Is the Way It Is and What You Can do About It:—Understanding the Universal Laws.* Virginia Beach, VA: A.R.E. Press, 1993.

McMoneagle, Joseph. *Remote Viewing Secrets: A Handbook.* Charlottesville, VA: Hampton Roads, 2000.

Melchizedec, Drunvalo. *Living in the Heart: How to Enter into the Sacred Space Within the Heart.* Flagstaff, AZ: Light Technology Publications, 2003.

Mellick, Jill. *The Art of Dreaming: Creative Tools for Dream Work.* New York: Gramercy Books, 2001.

Michaels, Ketherin, and Corvus Night. *The Experiment: An Exploration of Perception and Focus A Primer.* Santa Fe, NM: Greybear Publishing Co., 2002.

Michalko, Michael. *Cracking Creativity: The Secrets of Creative Genius.* Berkeley, CA: Ten Speed Press, 2001.

Millman, Dan. *Everyday Enlightenment: The Twelve Gateways to Personal Growth.* New York: Warner Books, 1999.

___. *The Laws of Spirit: A Tale of Transformation*. Novato, CA: New World Library, 2001.

___. *Living on Purpose: Straight Answers to Universal Questions*. Novato, CA: New World Library, 2000.

Mishlove, Jeffrey. *The Roots of Consciousness*. Tulsa, OK: Council Oak Books, 1993.

Monroe, Robert. *Journeys Out of the Body*. New York: Anchor-Doubleday, 1971.

Moody, Raymond A. *Life After Life*. Covington, GA: Mockingbird Books, 1975.

Mookerjee, Ajit. *Kundalini: Arousal of Inner Energy*. London: Thames and Hudson, 1982.

Moore, Thomas. *Care of the Soul: A Guide for Cultivating Depth & Sacredness in Everyday Life*. New York: Harper Collins, 1994.

___. *The Soul's Religion*. New York: Perennial, 2003.

Moss, Robert. *Conscious Dreaming: A Spiritual Path for Everyday Life*. New York: Three Rivers Press, 1996.

Mountain Dreamer, Oriah. *The Call: Discovering Why You Are Here*. New York: HarperCollins, 2003.

___. *The Dance: Moving to the Rhythms of Your True Self*. San Francisco: Harper SanFrancisco, 2001.

Murphy, Joseph. *The Cosmic Power Within You: Discover Your Unlimited Creative Potential and Set It Free*. Camarillo, CA: DeVorss, 2003.

Myss, Caroline. *Sacred Contracts: Awakening Your Divine Potential*. New York: Three Rivers Press, 2002.

Nelson, Martia. *Coming Home: The Return to True Self*. Novato, CA: Nataraj Publishing, 1995.

Neruda, Pablo. *Book of Questions*. Trans. William O'Daly, Port Townsend, WA: Copper Canyon Press, 2001.

Norris, Kathleen. *Amazing Grace: A Vocabulary of Faith*. New York: Riverhead Books, 1998.

Northrup, Suzane. *Everything Happens for a Reason: Love, Free Will and the Lessons of the Soul.* San Diego, CA: Jodere Group, 2002.

Okawa, Ryuho. *The Origin of Love: On the Beauty of Compassion.* New York: Lantern Books, 2003.

Orloff, Judith. *Second Sight.* New York: Warner, 1997.

Oslie, Pamala. *Make Your Dream Come True: Simple Steps for Changing the Beliefs That Limit You.* San Rafael, CA: Amber-Allen Publishing, 1998.

Ouspensky, P. D. *In Search of the Miraculous: Fragments of an Unknown Teaching.* New York: Harcourt, 2001.

Paddison, Sara. *The Hidden Power of the Heart: Discovering an Unlimited Source of Intelligence.* Boulder Creek, CA: Planetary Publications, 1998.

Paul, Stephen C. *Illuminations: Visions for Change, Growth, and Self-Acceptance.* San Francisco: Harper SanFrancisco, 1990.

Peace Pilgram. *Her Life and Works In Her Own Words.* Santa Fe: Ocean Tree Books, 1983.

Pearce, Joseph Chilton. *The Biology of Transcendence: A Blueprint for the Human Spirit.* Rochester, VT: Park Street Press, 2002.

Pearsall, Paul. *The Beethoven Factor: The New Positive Psychology of Hardiness, Happiness, Healing and Hope.* Charlottesville, VA: Hampton Roads, 2003.

___. *The Heart's Code: Tapping the Wisdom and Power of our Heart Energy.* New York: Broadway Books, 1999.

Pearson, Carol Lynn. *Consider the Butterfly: Transforming Your Life Through Meaningful Coincidence.* Layton, UT: Gibbs Smith, 2002.

Peck, M. Scott. *Further Along the Road Less Traveled.* New York: Simon & Schuster, 1993.

Perkins, John. *Shapeshifting: Shamanic Techniques for Global and Personal Transformation*. Rochester, VT: Inner Traditions, 1997.

Pierrakos, Eva. *The Pathwork of Self-Transformation*. New York: Bantam, 1990.

Piver, Susan. *The Hard Questions for an Authentic Life: 100 Essential Questions for Designing Your Life from the Inside Out*. New York: Gotham Books, 2004.

Prather, Hugh. *How to Live in the World and Still Be Happy*. Boston, MA: Conari, 2002.

Price, John Randolph. *Nothing Is Too Good to Be True*. Carlsbad, CA: Hay House, 2003.

Redfield, James, Michael Murphy, and Sylvia Timbers. *God and the Evolving Universe: The Next Step in Personal Evolution*. New York: Jeremy P. Tarcher, 2003.

Reed, Henry. *Awakening Your Psychic Powers*. New York: St. Martin's Press, 1996.

Richardson, Cheryl. *Take Time for Your Life*. New York: Broadway Books, 1998.

Roads, Michael J. *Journey Into Oneness*. Tiburon, CA: H.J. Kramer, 1994.

Roberts, Jane. *The Individual and the Nature of Mass Events*. San Rafael, CA: Amber-Allen Publishing, 1995.

___. *The Nature of Personal Reality: Specific, Practical Techniques for Solving Everyday Problems and Enriching the Life You Know*. San Rafael, CA: New World Library, 1994.

___. *Seth Speaks: The Eternal Validity of the Soul*. San Rafael, CA: New World Library, 1994.

Robertson, Robin. *Mining the Soul: From the Inside Out*. York Beach, ME: Nicolas-Hays, 2000.

Robinson, Lynn. *Compass Of The Soul: 52 Ways Intuition Can Guide You To The Life Of Your Dreams*. Kansas City, MO: Andrews McMeel Publishing, 2003.

_____. *Divine Intuition: Your Guide to Creating a Life You Love*. New York: DK Publishing, 2001.

Roman, Sanaya. *Spiritual Growth: Being Your Higher Self*. Tiburon, CA: HJ Kramer, 1989.

Roth, Ron, and Peter Occhiogrosso. *Reclaim Your Spiritual Power*. Carlsbad, CA: Hay House, 2002.

Rother, Steve. *Re-member: a Handbook for Human Evolution*. Poway, CA: Lightworker Publications, 2000.

Ruiz, Don Miguel. *The Four Agreements: A Practical Guide to Personal Freedom*. San Rafael, CA: Amber-Allen Publishing, 1997.

Russell, Peter. *From Science to God: A Physicist's Journey into the Mystery of Consciousness*. Novato, CA: New World Library, 2003.

Sagan, Samuel. *Awakening the Third Eye*. Sydney: Clairvision School Foundation, 1997.

Saint-Exupéry, Antoine de. *The Little Prince*. Trans. K. Woods. 1943; reprint, San Diego, CA: Harcourt Brace Jovanovich, 1971.

Salzberg, Sharon. *Loving Kindness*. Boston: Shambhala, 1995.

Sams, Jamie. *Dancing the Dream: The Seven Sacred Paths Of Human Transformation*. New York: HarperCollins, 1999.

Satprem. *The Mind of the Cells*. New York: Institute for Evolutionary Research, 1982.

Shield, Benjamin, and Richard Carlson, eds. *For the Love of God: Handbook for the Spirit*. Novato, CA: New World Library, 1997.

Shumsky, Susan G. *Divine Revelation*. New York: Fireside, 1996.

Sky, Michael. *The Power of Emotion: Using Your Emotional Energy to Transform Your Life*. Rochester, VT: Inner Traditions, 2003.

Small, Jacqueline. *Psyche's Seeds: The 12 Sacred Principles of Soul-Based Psychology*. Los Angeles: Jeremy P. Tarcher, 2001.

Spalding, Baird T. *Life and Teachings of the Masters of the Far East*. Marina Del Rey, CA: DeVorss, 1996.

Spangler, David. *Blessing: The Art and the Practice*. New York: Riverhead, 2002.

Sparrowdancer, Mary. *The Love Song of the Universe*. Charlottesville, VA: Hampton Roads, 2001.

Steinem, Gloria. *Revolution from Within: A Book of Self-Esteem* Boston: Little, Brown and Company, 1992.

Steiner, Rudolf. *Intuitive Thinking as a Spiritual Path*. Trans. Michael Lipson. Great Barrington, MA: Anthroposophic Press, 1995.

Stepanek, Mattie J. T. *Loving Through Heartsongs*. New York: Hyperion, 2003.

Stepaniak, Joanne. *Compassionate Living for Healing, Wholeness, and Harmony*. Lincolnwood, IL: Keats Publishing, 2001.

Stephan, Naomi. *Finding Your Life Mission: How to Unleash That Creative Power and Live with Intention*. Walpole, NH: Stillpoint, 1990.

Stephens, Jose. *Transforming Your Dragons: Turning Personality Fear Patterns into Personal Power*. Santa Fe: Bear & Co., 1994.

Strassman, Rick. *DMT: The Spirit Molecule: A Doctor's Revolutionary Research into the Biology of Near-Death and Mystical Experiences*. Rochester, VT: Inner Traditions, 2001.

Swimme, Brian. *The Universe Is a Green Dragon: A Cosmic Creation Story*. Santa Fe, NM: Bear & Co, 1988.

Tappe, Nancy Ann. *Understanding Your Life Through Color*. Carlsbad, CA: Starling Publishers, 1982.

Tart, Charles. *Mind Science: Meditation Training for Practical People*. Boston: Wisdom 2000.

___. *Waking Up: Overcoming the Obstacles to Human Potential.* Boston: Shambhala, 1987.

Taylor, Susan L. *Lessons in Living.* New York: Anchor Books, 1995.

Taylor, Terry Lynn. *Creating With the Angels.* Tiburon, CA: H J Kramer Inc., 1993.

Thompson Smith, Angela. *Remote Perceptions: Out-of-Body Experiences, Remote Viewing, and Other Normal Abilities.* Charlottesville, VA: Hampton Roads, 1998.

Thurman, Robert. *Infinite Life: Living Here and Now, Beyond and Forever.* New York: Riverhead, 2004.

Tillich, Paul. *The Eternal Now.* New York: Charles Scribner's Sons, 1956.

Todeschi, Kevin J. *Soul Development.* Virginia Beach, VA: A.R.E. Press, 2000.

Tolle, Eckhart. *The Power of Now: A Guide to Spiritual Enlightenment.* Vancouver, Canada, Namaste Publishing, 1997.

___ *Stillness Speaks.* Novato, CA: New World Library; 2003.

Trine, Ralph Waldo. *In Tune With the Infinite.* Richmond, VA: Oklea Press, 2003.

Ullman, M., Stanley Krippner, and A. Vaughan. *Dream Telepathy.* New York: Macmillan, 1973.

Ueshiba, Morihei. *The Art of Peace.* Boston: Shambhala, 1992.

Vanzant, Iyanla. *One Day My Soul Just Opened Up: 40 Days And 40 Nights Toward Spiritual Strength And Personal Growth.* New York: Fireside, 1998.

___. *Until Today! Daily Devotions for Spiritual Growth and Peace of Mind.* New York: Simon & Schuster, 2000.

Wagner, David. *Life As a Daymaker: How to Change the World by Simply Making Someone's Day.* San Diego, CA: Jodere, 2003.

Wakefield, Dan. *Expect a Miracle: The Miraculous Things That Happen to Ordinary People*. New York: Harper, 1998.

Wallace, B Allan. *Choosing Reality*. Ithaca, NY: Snow Lion, 2003.

Walsh, Neale Donald. *Conversations With God: An Uncommon Dialogue*. New York: Putnam, 1999.

___.*Tomorrow's God: Our Greatest Spiritual Challenge*. New York: Atria, 2003.

Walsh, Roger. *Essential Spirituality: The 7 Central Practices to Awaken Heart and Mind*. New York: John Wiley & Sons, 2000.

Walters, Donald. *Awaken to Superconciousness: How to Use Meditation for Inner Peace, Intuitive Guidance, and Greater Awareness*. Nevada City, CA: Crystal Clarity Publishers, 2000.

Warren, Neil C. *Make Anger Your Ally: Harnessing Our Most Baffling Emotion*. Garden City, NY: Doubleday, 1983.

Warren, Rick. *The Purpose-Driven Life: What on Earth Am I Here For?* Grand Rapids, MI: Zondervan, 2002.

Watts, Alan. *The Wisdom of Insecurity*. New York: Vintage, 1968.

Weiss, Brian L. *Many Lives, Many Masters*. New York: Fireside, 1988.

___. *Messages from the Masters: Tapping into the Power of Love*. New York: Warner, 2001.

Wesselman, Hank. *The Journey to the Sacred Garden: A Guide to Traveling in the Spiritual Realms*. Carlsbad, CA: Hay House, 2003.

West, Melissa Gayle. *Exploring the Labyrinth: A Guide for Healing and Spiritual Growth*. New York: Broadway, 2000.

Wilber, Ken. *A Brief History of Everything*. Boston, MA: Shambhala, 2001.

___. *No Boundary: Eastern and Western Approaches to Personal Growth*. Boston: Shambhala, 2001.

Wilde, Stuart. *Infinite Self: 33 Steps to Reclaiming Your Inner Power*. Carlsbad, CA: Hay House, 1996.

___. *Miracles*. Carlsbad, CA: Hay House, 1998.

Williamson, Marianne. *A Return to Love: Reflections on the Principles of A Course In Miracles*. New York: HarperCollins, 1992.

Wolman, Richard N. *Thinking With Your Soul: Spiritual Intelligence and Why It Matters*. New York: Harmony, 2001.

Woolf, Vernon V. *Holodynamics: How to Develop and Manage Your Personal Power*. Tucson, AZ: Harbinger House, 1990.

Wright, Machaelle Small. *Behaving As If the God In All Life Mattered*. Warrenton, VA: Perelandra Ltd., 1997.

Zoglio, Suzanne. *Create A Life That Tickles Your Soul: Finding Peace, Passion, & Purpose*. Doylestown, PA: Tower Hill Press, 2000.

Zukav, Gary. *The Seat of the Soul*. New York: Simon & Schuster, 1989.

Zukav, Gary, and Linda Francis. *The Heart of the Soul: Emotional Awareness*. New York, Simon & Schuster, 2002.

Relationships

Aron, Elaine N. *The Highly Sensitive Person in Love: Understanding and Managing Relationships When the World Overwhelms You.* New York: Broadway Books, 2001.

Blanchard, Kenneth, et al. *Whale Done! The Power of Positive Relationships.* New York: Free Press, 2002.

Bolt, Carol. *Love's Book of Answers.* New York: Stewart, Tabori & Chang, 2002.

Brandon, Nathaniel. *Honoring the Self: Self-Esteem and Personal Tranformation.* New York: Bantam, 1985.

Brehony, Kathleen. *Living A Connected Life: Creating and Maintaining Relationships that Last a Lifetime.* New York: Owl Books, 2003.

Brenner, Helene. *I Know I'm in There Somewhere: A Woman's Guide to Finding Her Inner Voice and Living a Life of Authenticity.* New York: Gotham Books, 2003.

Browne, Sylvia and Lindsay Harrison. *Past Lives, Future Healing: A Psychic Reveals the Secrets to Good Health and Great Relationships.* New York: New American Library, 2002.

Carlson, Kristine, and Richard Carlson. *Don't Sweat the Small Stuff in Love: Simple Ways to Nurture and Strengthen Your Relationships While Avoiding the Habits That Break Down Your Loving Connection.* New York: Hyperion, 2000.

Carter, Steven, and Julia Sokol. *He's Scared, She's Scared: Understanding the Hidden Fears That Sabotage Your Relationships.* New York: DTP, 1995.

Cohen, Alan. *Happily Even After: Can You Be Friends After Lovers.* Carlsbad, CA: Hay House, 1999.

___. *Rising in Love: Opening Your Heart in All Your Relationships.* Carlsbad, CA: Hay House, 1996.

Eisler, Riane, *The Power of Partnership: Seven Relationships That Will Change Your Life*. Novato, CA: New World Library, 2003.

Ferrini, Paul. *Creating a Spiritual Relationship: A Guide to Growth & Happiness for Couples on the Path*. Greenfield, MA: Heartways Press, 2000.

___. *Dancing With the Beloved: Opening Our Hearts to the Lessons of Love*. Greenfield, MA: Heartways Press, 2001.

Fisher, Bruce, and Nina Hart. *Loving Choices: An Experience in Growing Relationships*. Atascadero, CA: Impact Publishers, 2000.

Fisher, Helen, *Why We Love: The Nature and Chemistry of Romantic Love*. New York: Henry Holt, 2004.

Ford, Debbie. *Spiritual Divorce: Divorce As a Catalyst for an Extraordinary Life*. San Francisco: Harper SanFrancisco, 2001.

Freston, Kathy. *Expect a Miracle: 7 Spiritual Steps to Finding the Right Relationship*. New York: St. Martin's Press, 2003.

Gold, Taro. *What Is Love? A Simple Buddhist Guide To Romantic Happiness*. Kansas City, MO. Andrews McMeel Publishing, 2003.

Goodbread, Joseph. *Radical Intercourse: How Dreams Unite Us In Love, Conflict and Other Inevitable Relationships*. Portland, OR: Lao Tse Press, 1997.

Gorski, Terence T. *Getting Love Right: Learning the Choices of Healthy Intimacy*. New York: Fireside, 1993.

Gottman, John M. *The Relationship Cure: A 5-Step Guide to Strengthening Your Marriage, Family, and Friendships*. New York: Three Rivers Press, 2002.

Gottman, John M., and Nan Silver. *The Seven Principles for Making Marriage Work: A Practical Guide from the Country's Foremost Relationship Expert*. New York: Three Rivers Press, 2000.

Gray, John. *Mars and Venus Starting Over: A Practical Guide for Finding Love Again After a Painful Breakup, Divorce, or the Loss of a Loved One*. New York: Quill, 2002.

Goulston, Mark, and Philip Goldberg. *The 6 Secrets of a Lasting Relationship: How to Fall in Love Again-And Stay There*. New York: Perigee, 2002.

Harrison, Steven. *Being One: Finding Our Self in Relationship*. Boulder, CO: Sentient Publications, 2002.

Hendricks, Gay. *Conscious Loving: The Journey to Co-Commitment*. New York: Bantam, 1992.

Hendricks, Kathlyn, and Gay Hendricks. *The Conscious Heart: Seven Soul-Choices That Inspire Creative Partnership*. New York: Bantam, 1999.

Hendrix, Harville. *Getting the Love You Want: A Guide for Couples*. New York: Owl Books, 2001.

Heyneman, Nicolas E. *Dreams & Relationships: Interpret Your Dreams, Understand Your Emotions, and Find Fulfillment*. San Francisco: Chronicle Books, 2000.

Huber, Cheri. *Be the Person You Want to Find: Relationship and Self-Discovery*. Murphys, CA: Keep It Simple Books, 1997.

Johnson, Kelly E. *A Relationship for a Lifetime: Everything You Need to Know to Create a Love That Lasts*. Carlsbad, CA: Hay House, 2001.

Joudry, Patricia and Maurie Pressman. *Twin Souls: Finding Your True Spiritual Partner*. Center City, MN: Hazelden, 2000.

Kasl, Charlotte. *If the Buddha Dated: A Handbook for Finding Love on a Spiritual Path*. New York: Penguin Putnam, 1999.

Kingma, Daphne Rose. *The Future of Love: The Power of the Soul in Intimate Relationships*. New York: Main Street Books, 1999.

Lerner, Harriet. *The Dance of Connection: How to Talk to Someone When You're Mad, Hurt, Scared, Frustrated, Insulted, Betrayed, or Desperate*. New York: Quill, 2002.

McGraw, Phillip C. *Relationship Rescue: A Seven-Step Strategy for Reconnectng With Your Partner*. New York: Hyperion Press, 2000.

Miller, Carolyn Godschild. *Soulmates: Following Inner Guidance to the Relationship of Your Dreams*. Tiburon, CA: HJ Kramer, 2000.

Moore, Thomas. *Soul Mates: Honoring the Mysteries of Love and Relationship*. New York: HarperPerennial, 1994.

Morrissey, Mary Manin. *No Less Than Greatness: The Seven Spiritual Principles That Make Real Love Possible*. New York: Bantam Books, 2001.

Niven, David. *100 Simple Secrets of Great Relationships: What Scientists Have Learned and How You Can Use It*. San Francisco: Harper SanFrancisco, 2003.

Page, Susan. *How One of You Can Bring the Two of You Together: Breakthrough Strategies to Resolve Your Conflicts and Reignite Your Love*. New York: Broadway, 1998.

Prather, Gayle and Hugh Prather. *A Book of Couples*. New York: MJF Books, 2001.

___. *I Will Never Leave You: How Couples Can Achieve The Power Of Lasting Love*. New York: Bantam, 1996.

Psaris, Jett, and Marlena S. Lyons. *Undefended Love: The way that you felt about yourself when you first fell in love is the way that you can feel all the time*. Oakland, CA: New Harbinger Publications, 2000.

Raffel, Steve. *Should I Stay Or Go? How Controlled Separation (CS) Can Save Your Marriage*. Chicago, IL: McGraw-Hill-Contemporary Books, 1999.

Real, Terrence. *How Can I Get Through to You: Reconnecting Men and Women.* New York: Scribner, 2002.

Richo, David. *How to Be an Adult in Relationships: The Five Keys to Mindful Loving.* Boston: Shambhala. 2002.

Richards, Charles. *Karmic Relationships.* San Diego, CA: Jodere, 2002.

Robinson, Jonathan. *Communication Miracles for Couples: Easy and Effective Tools to Create More Love and Less Conflict.* Boston, MA: Conari, 1997.

Rockwell, Irini. *The Five Wisdom Energies: A Buddhist Way of Understanding Personalities, Emotions, and Relationships.* Boston: Shambhala, 2002.

Rodgers, Beverly, and Tom Rodgers. *How to Find Mr. or Ms. Right: A Practical Guide to Finding a Soul Mate.* San Jose, CA: Resource Publications, 1999.

Rosen, Mark I. *Thank You for Being Such a Pain: Spiritual Guidance for Dealing With Difficult People.* New York: Three Rivers Press, 1999.

Rosenberg, Marshall B. *Nonviolent Communication: A Language of Life: Create Your Life, Your Relationships, and Your World in Harmony with Your Values.* Encinitas, CA: PuddleDancer Press, 2003.

Ruiz, Don Miguel. *The Mastery of Love: A Practical Guide to the Art of Relationship.* San Rafael, CA: Amber-Allen Publishing, 1999.

Ryan, M. J. *Attitudes of Gratitude in Love: Creating More Joy in Your Relationship.* Berkeley, CA: Conari Press, 2002.

Rushnell, SQuire. *When God Winks on Love: Let the Power of Coincidence Lead You to Love.* New York: Atria, 2004.

Ryan, M. J. *Attitudes of Gratitude in Love: Creating More Joy in Your Relationship.* Berkeley, CA: Conari Press, 2002.

Sato, Toru. *The Ever-Transcending Spirit: The Psychology of Human Relationships, Consciousness, and Development.* Lincoln, NE: iUniverse, Inc., 2003.

Schlessinger, Laura C. *Ten Stupid Things Couples Do to Mess Up Their Relationships.* New York: Quill, 2002.

Scire, Anthony C. *The Power of 2: Win Big with People in Your Work and in Life.* Hummelstown, PA: Possibility Press, 2002.

Shoshanna, Brenda. *Zen and the Art of Falling in Love.* New York: Simon & Schuster, 2003.

Stone, Hal. and Sidra Stone. *Embracing Each Other: Relationship As Teacher, Healer and Guide.* Novato, CA: New World Library, 2000.

Thoele, Sue Patton. *Heart Centered Marriage: Fulfilling Our Natural Desire for Sacred Partnership.* Berkeley, CA: Conari Press, 1996.

Tomioka, Ariel. *On the Breath of the Gods: A Journey Into the Heart of Love.* Carmichael, CA: Helios House, 1994.

Vanzant, Iyanla. *In the Meantime: Finding Yourself and the Love You Want.* New York: Fireside, 1999.

___. *Love and Awakening: Discovering the Sacred Path of Intimate Relationship.* New York: Harper Collins, 1996.

Walters, J. Donald. *Expansive Marriage: A Way to Self-Realization.* Nevada City, CA: Crystal Clarity Publishers, 2003.

Weiss, Brian L. *Only Love is Real: A Story of Soulmates Reunited.* New York: Warner, 1997.

Welwood, John. *Journey of the Heart: The Path of Conscious Love.* New York: HarperPerennial, 1996.

Williamson, Marianne. *Enchanted Love: The Mystical Power Of Intimate Relationships.* New York: Touchstone, 2001.

Wisdom, Susan, and Jennifer Green. *Stepcoupling: Creating and Sustaining a Strong Marriage in Today's Blended Family.* New York: Three Rivers Press, 2002.

Business/Leadership/Success

Albion, Mark. *Making a Life, Making a Living: Reclaiming Your Purpose and Passion In Business and In Life*. New York: Warner, 2000.

Albrecht, Karl. *Corporate Radar: Tracking the Forces that Are Shaping Your Business*. New York: Amacom, 2000.

Allen, Marc. *Visionary Business: An Entrepreneur's Guide to Success*. Novato, CA: New World Library, 1997.

Autry, James A., and Stephen Mitchell. *Real Power: Business Lessons from the Tao te Ching*. New York: Penguin/Putnam, 1998.

Biggs, Richard K. *Burn Brightly Without Burning Out: Balancing Your Career with the Rest of Your Life*. Nashville, TN: Thomas Nelson, 2003.

Bissonnette, Denise. *The Wholehearted Journey: Bringing Qualities of Soul to Everyday Life and Work*. Santa Cruz, CA: Diversity World, 2002.

Blanchard, Kenneth H. *The Heart of a Leader*. Colorado Springs, CO: Honor Books, 1998.

Boldt, Laurence G. *Zen and the Art of Making a Living: A Practical Guide to Creative Career Design*. New York: Penguin USA, 1999.

Bornstein, David. *How to Change the World: Social Entrepreneurs and the Power of New Ideas*. New York: Oxford University Press, 2004.

Brandon, Nathaniel. *Self Esteem at Work*. San Francisco: Jossey-Bass, 1998.

Brinckerhoff, Peter C. *Social Entrepreneurship: The Art of Mission-Based Venture Development*. New York: John Wiley & Sons, 2000.

Brown, Frederick S. *Money and Spirit: Creating a New Consciousness in Making and Managing Your Money.* Virginia Beach, VA: A.R.E. Press, 1995.

Bstan-'dzin-rgya-mtsho, Dalai Lama XIV, and Howard C. Cutler. *The Art of Happiness at Work.* New York: Riverhead, 2003.

Buckingham, Marcus, and Donald O. Clifton. *Now, Discover Your Strengths.* New York: Free Press, 2001.

Butterworth, Eric. *Spiritual Economics: The Principles and Process of True Prosperity.* Unity Village, MO: Unity, 1998.

Carlson, Richard. *Don't Sweat the Small Stuff At Work: Simple Ways to Minimize Stress & Conflict While Bringing Out the Best In Yourself and Others.* New York: Hyperion, 1998.

Chopra, Deepak. *The Seven Spiritual Laws of Success: A Practical Guide to the Fulfillment of Your Dreams.* Novato, CA: Amber-Allen Publishing, 1995.

Collins, James C., and Jerry I. Porras. *Built to Last: Successful Habits of Visionary Companies.* New York: HarperBusiness, 1994.

Covey, Stephen R. *Principle Centered Leadership.* New York: Simon & Schuster, 1992.

Csikszentmihalyi, Mihaly. *Good Business: Leadership, Flow, and the Making of Meaning.* New York: Viking Press, 2003.

Deslauriers, Paul. *In the High-Energy Zone: The 6 Characteristics of Highly Effective Groups.* Makawao, HI: Inner Ocean Publishing, 2002.

Ehringer, Ann Graham. *Make Up Your Mind: Entrepreneurs Talk About Decision Making.* Santa Monica, CA: Merritt Publishing, 1995.

Flick, Deborah L. *From Debate to Dialogue: Using the Understanding Process to Transform Our Conversations*. Boulder: Orchid Publications, 1998.

Fox, Matthew. *The Reinvention of Work: A New Vision of Livelihood for Our Time*. New York: HarperCollins, 1994.

Frances, Tarin. *Magical Quest: Six Steps to Career Success*. Long Beach, CA: Sirene Impressions, 2000.

Garfield, Charles, et al., eds. *The Soul of Business*. Carlsbad, CA: Hay House, 1997.

Gladwell, Malcolm. *The Tipping Point: How Little Things Can Make a Big Difference*. New York: Back Bay Books, 2002.

Glouberman, Dina. *Joy of Burnout: How the End of the World Can Be a New Beginning*. London: Hodder & Stoughton, 2002.

Goleman, Daniel. *Working With Emotional Intelligence*. New York: Bantam, 2000.

Goleman, Daniel, Richard Boyatzis, and Annie McKee. *Primal Leadership: Realizing the Power of Emotional Intelligence*. Boston: Harvard Business School Press, 2002.

Graves, Stephen R., and Thomas G. Addington. *Clout: Tapping Spiritual Wisdom to Become a Person of Influence*. San Francisco: Jossey-Bass, 2003.

Griffin, Emilie. *The Reflective Executive: A Spirituality of Business and Enterprise*. New York: Crossroad, 1993.

Guillory, William A. *The Living Organization: Spirituality in the Workplace: A Guide for Adapting to the Chaotically Changing Workplace*. Salt Lake City: Innovations International, 2000.

Hall, Andria. *The Walk at Work: Seven Steps to Spiritual Success on the Job*. Colorado Springs, CO: Waterbrook Press, 2003.

Handy, Charles. *Beyond Certainty: The Changing World of Organizations*. Boston: Harvard Business School Press, 1996.

Hansen, Mark Victor, and Robert G. Allen. *The One Minute Millionaire: The Enlightened Way to Wealth*. New York: Harmony Books, 2002.

Harrow, Susan. *Sell Yourself Without Selling Your Soul: A Woman's Guide to Promoting Herself, Her Business, Her Product, or Her Cause with Integrity and Spirit*. New York: HarperResource, 2003.

Hawkin, Paul. *The Ecology of Commerce: A Declaration of Sustainability*. New York: Harper Business, 1994.

Hawkins, Kathleen L. *Spirit Incorporated: How to Follow Your Spiritual Path from 9 to 5*. Marina del Rey, CA: DeVorss & Company, 1998.

Hendricks, Gay, and Kate Ludeman. *The Corporate Mystic: A Guidebook for Visionaries With Their Feet on the Ground*. New York: Bantam, 1997.

Houlder, Dominic J., and Kulananda Houlder. *Mindfulness and Money: The Buddhist Path to Abundance*. New York: Broadway, 2003.

Isaacs, William. *Dialogue and the Art of Thinking Together: A Pioneering Approach to Communicating in Business and in Life*. New York: Doubleday, 1999.

Jaeger, Barrie S. *Making Work Work for the Highly Sensitive Person*. New York: McGraw-Hill, 2003.

Jaworski, Joseph. *Synchronicity: The Inner Path of Leadership*. San Francisco, CA: Barrett-Koehler, 1998.

Johnson, Spencer. *The Present: The Gift That Makes You Happier And More Successful At Work And In Life, Today!* New York: Doubleday, 2003.

Johnston, Robert K., and J. Walker Smith. *Life Is Not Work, Work Is Not Life: Simple Reminders for Finding Balance in a 24/7 World*. Berkeley, CA: Wildcat Canyon Press, 2001.

Kahaner, Larry. *Values, Prosperity, and the Talmud: Business Lessons from the Ancient Rabbis*. Hoboken, NJ: John Wiley & Sons, 2003.

Klein, Eric, and John B. Izzo. *Awakening Corporate Soul: Four Paths to Unleash the Power of People at Work*. Gloucester, MA: Fair Winds Press, 1999.

Kushner, Harold S. *Living a Life That Matters: Resolving the Conflict Between Conscience and Success*. New York: Alfred A. Knopf, 2001.

Larson, Cynthia Sue. *Aura Advantage: How the Colors in Your Aura Can Help You Attain What You Desire and Attract Success*. Avon, MA: Adams Media Corporation, 2003.

Leider, Richard J., and David A. Shapiro. *Whistle While You Work: Heeding Your Life's Calling*. San Francisco: Berrett-Koehler Publishing, 2001.

Leonard, George. *Mastery: The Keys to Success and Long-Term Fulfillment*. New York: Plume, 1992.

Loehr, Jim, and Tony Schwartz. *The Power of Full Engagement: Managing Energy, Not Time, is the Key to High Performance and Personal Renewal*. New York: Free Press, 2003.

Low, Jonathan, and Pam Cohen Kalafut. *Invisible Advantage: How Intangibles are Driving Business Performance*. Cambridge, MA: Perseus Publishing, 2002.

Marcic, Dorothy. *Managing with the Wisdom of Love: Uncovering Virtue in People and Organizations*. San Francisco: Jossey-Bass, 1997.

Maxwell, John C. *Thinking for a Change: 11 Ways Highly Successful People Approach Life and Work*. New York: Warner, 2003.

McGraw, Phillip C. *Life Strategies: Doing What Works, Doing What Matters*. New York: Hyperion, 2000.

McNeal, Reggie. *A Work of Heart: Understanding How God Shapes Spiritual Leaders*. San Francisco: Jossey-Bass, 2000.

Menter, Marcia. *Office Sutras: Exercises for Your Soul at Work*. Boston: Red Wheel, 2003.

Orman, Suze. *The Courage to be Rich: Creating a Life of Material and Spiritual Abundance*. New York: Penguin Putnam, 2001.

___. *9 Steps to Financial Freedom: Practical and Spiritual Steps So You Can Stop Worrying*. New York: Three Rivers Press, 2000.

Osterberg, Rolf. *Corporate Renaissance: Business as an Adventure in Human Development*. New York: Paraview Special Editions, 2003.

Palmer, Parker J. *Let Your Life Speak: Listening for the Voice of Vocation*. San Francisco: Jossey-Bass, 2000.

Pearsall, Paul. *Toxic Success: How to Stop Striving and Start Thriving*. Makawao, HI: Inner Ocean Publishing, 2002.

Peppers, Cheryl and Alan Briskin. *Bringing Your Soul to Work: An Everyday Practice*. San Francisco: Berrett-Koehler, 2000.

Peters, Tom. *Re-imagine!* New York: DK Publications, 2003.

Ponder, Catherine. *Dynamic Laws of Prosperity*. Camarillo, CA: DeVorss & Company, 1988.

Rechtschaffen, Stephen. *Time Shifting: Creating More Time to Enjoy Your Life*. New York: Doubleday, 1997.

Renesch, John E. *Getting To The Better Future: A Matter of Conscious Choosing: How Business Can Lead the Way to New Possibilities*. San Francisco: New Business Books, 2000.

Richmond, Lewis. *Work As a Spiritual Practice: A Practical Buddhist Approach to Inner Growth and Satisfaction on the Job*. New York: Broadway Books, 2000.

Roach, Michael. *The Diamond Cutter: The Buddha on Strategies for Managing Your Business and Your Life*. New York: Doubleday, 2000.

Robinson, Jonathan. *Real Wealth: A Spiritual Approach to Money and Work*. Carlsbad, CA: Hay House, 1998.

Robinson, Lynn A. *Real Prosperity: Using the Power of Intuition to Create Financial and Spiritual Abundance*. Kansas City, MO: Andrews McMeel Publishing, 2004.

Saks, Claude. *Spirituality for the Business Person: Inner Practices for Success*. Santa Fe: Heartsfire Books, 1998.

Saltzman, Amy. *Downshifting: Reinventing Success on a Slower Track*. New York: HarperCollins, 1991.

Scheinfeld, Robert. *The Invisible Path to Success: Seven Steps to Understanding and Managing the Unseen Forces Shaping Your Life*. Charlottesville, VA: Hampton Roads, 2003.

Seger, Linda. *Web Thinking: Connecting, Not Competing, for Success*. Makawao, HI: Inner Ocean Publishing, 2002.

Senge, Peter, C. Otto Scharmer, Joseph Jaworski, and Betty Sue Flowers. *Presence: Human Purpose and the Field of the Future*. Cambridge, MA: Sol, 2004.

Sharma, Robin S. *Leadership Wisdom from the Monk Who Sold His Ferrari: The 8 Rituals of Visionary Leaders*. Carlsbad, CA: Hay House, 2003.

Sher, Barbara. *Live the Life You Love: In Ten Easy Step-By Step Lessons*. New York: Dell, 1996.

Shinn, Florence Scovel. *The Wisdom of Florence Scovel Shinn*, (Includes four complete books: *The Game of Life and How to Play It; The Power of the Spoken Word; Your Word Is Your Wand; The Secret of Success.*) New York: Fireside/Simon & Schuster, 1989.

Sinetar, Marsha. *Do What You Love, the Money Will Follow: Discovering Your Right Livelihood.* New York: DTP, 1989.

___. *To Build the Life You Want, Create the Work You Love: The Spiritual Dimension of Entrepreneuring.* New York: St. Martin's Press, 1996.

Smith, Frederick W. *The Book of Leadership Wisdom.* Peter Krauss, ed. New York: John Wiley & Sons, 1998.

Stevens, Jose, and Lena Stevens. *The Power Path: The Shaman's Way to Success in Business and Life.* Novato, CA: New World Library, 2002.

Tapscott, Don, David Ticoll, and Alex Lowy. *Digital Capital: Harnessing the Power of Business Webs.* Watertown, MA: Harvard Business School Press, 2000.

Ury, William. *Getting Past No: Negotiating Your Way from Confrontation to Cooperation.* New York: Bantam, 1993.

Vitale, Joseph. *Spiritual Marketing: A Proven 5-Step Formula for Easily Creating Wealth from the Inside Out.* Bloomington, IN: 1stBooks Library, 2002.

Wheatley, Margaret J. *A Simpler Way.* San Francisco, CA: Berrett-Koehler, 1998.

Wilber, Ken. *A Theory of Everything: An Integral Vision for Business, Politics, Science and Spirituality.* Boston: Shambhala, 2001.

Witten, Dona, and Akong Tulku Rinpoche. *Enlightened Management: Bringing Buddhist Principles to Work.* Rochester, VT: Park Street Press, 1999.

New Science

Abbott, Edwin A. *Flatland: A Romance of Many Dimensions*. Mineola, NY: Dover, 1992.

Abraham, Ralph, Terence McKenna, and Rupert Sheldrake. *Trialogues at the Edge of the West: Chaos, Creativity, and the Resacralization of the World*. Santa Fe: Bear & Co., 1992.

Ashton, Anthony. *Harmonograph: A Visual Guide to the Mathematics of Music*. New York: Walker & Co., 2003.

Barabási, Albert-László. *Linked: How Everything Is Connected to Everything Else and What It Means*. New York: Plume, 2003.

Barrow. John D. *The Book of Nothing: Vacuums, Voids, and the Latest Ideas About the Origins of the Universe*. New York: Vintage, 2002.

___. *The Constants of Nature: From Alpha to Omega—The Numbers That Encode the Deepest Secrets of the Universe*. New York: Pantheon Books, 2003.

Becker. Robert O., and Gary Selden. *The Body Electric: Electromagnetism and the Foundation of Life*. London: Quill-William Morrow. 1985.

Bohm, David. *On Dialogue*. Lee Nichol, Ed. New York: Routledge, 2000.

___. *Wholeness and the Implicate Order*. New York: Routledge, 2002.

Braud, William. *Distant Mental Influence: Its Contributions to Science, Healing, and Human Interactions*. Charlottesville, VA: Hampton Roads, 2003.

Brennan, J. H. *Time Travel: A New Perspective*. St. Paul, Minnesota: Llewellyn, 1997.

Briggs, John. *Fractals: The Patterns of Chaos*. New York: Simon & Schuster, 1993.

Briggs, John, and F. David Peat. *Seven Life Lessons of Chaos: Spiritual Wisdom from the Science of Change.* New York: Harper Perennial, 2000.

Brown, Guy C. *The Energy of Life: The Science of What Makes Our Minds and Bodies Work.* New York: Free Press-Simon & Schuster, 1999.

Buchanan. Mark. *Ubiquity: Why Catastrophes Happen.* New York: Three Rivers Press, 2002.

Capra, Fritjof. *The Tao of Physics: An Exploration of the Parallels Between Modern Physics and Eastern Mysticism.* Boston: Shambhala, 2000.

___. *The Web of Life: A New Understanding of Living Systems.* New York: Doubleday, 1997.

Churchland, P.S. *Neurophilosophy: Towards a Unified Science of the Mind/Brain.* Cambridge: MIT Press, 1986.

Cohen, Andrew. *Living Enlightenment: A Call for Evolution Beyond Ego.* Lenox, MA: Moksha Press, 2002.

Cole, K.C. *The Hole in the Universe: How Scientists Peered over the Edge of Emptiness and Found Everything.* San Diego, CA: Harcourt, Inc., 2001.

Combs, Allan, et al. *Synchronicity: Through the Eyes of Science, Myth and the Trickster.* New York: Marlowe & Company, 2000.

Crandall, B.C., ed. *Nanotechnology: Molecular Speculations on Global Abundance.* Cambridge: MIT Press, 1996.

Crick, F.H.C. *The Astonishing Hypothesis: The Scientific Search For the Soul.* London: Simon & Simon, 1994.

Davidson, John. *The Secret of the Creative Vacuum: Man and the Energy Dance.* Saffron Walden: C.W. Daniel, 1989.

___. *Subtle Energy.* Saffron Walden: C. W. Daniel, 1987.

Davies, Paul, and John Gribbon. *The Matter Myth: Dramatic Discoveries That Challenge Our Understanding of Physical Reality*. New York: Touchstone Books, 1992.

Dennett, Daniel C. *Consciousness Explained*. London: Allen Lane/Penguin, 1991.

Dossey, Larry. *Recovering the Soul: A Scientific and Spiritual Search*. New York: Bantam, 1989.

Friedman, Norman. *Bridging Science and Spirit: Common Elements in David Bohm's Physics, the Perennial Philosophy and Seth*. Needham, MA: Moment Point Press, 1994.

Feynman, Richard Phillips, et al. *Six Not-So-Easy Pieces: Einstein's Relativity, Symmetry, and Space-Time*. New York: Perseus Publishing, 1998.

Fox, Matthew, and Rupert Sheldrake. *The Physics of Angels: Exploring the Realm Where Science and Spirit Meet*. San Francisco: HarperSan Francisco, 1996.

Gazzaniga, M.S. *Mind Matters: How Mind and Brain Interact To Create Our Conscious Lives*. Boston: Houghton Mifflin, 1988.

Gerrald, David. *The Man Who Folded Himself*. Dallas, TX: BenBella Books, 2003.

Gilovich, Thomas. *How We Know What Isn't So: The Fallibility of Human Reason In Everyday Life*. New York: Free Press, 1993.

Gleick, James. *Chaos: Making a New Science*. Placerville, CA: Gold Leaf Press, 1987.

___. *Faster: The Acceleration of Just About Everything*. New York: Pantheon Books, 1999.

Goswami, Amit. *Physics of the Soul: The Quantum Book of Living, Dying, Reincarnation and Immortality*. Charlottesville, VA: Hampton Roads, 2001.

Goswami, Maggie, et al. *The Self-Aware Universe: How Consciousness Creates the Material World.* Los Angeles: Jeremy P. Tarcher, 1995.

Greene, Brian. *The Elegant Universe: Superstrings, Hidden Dimensions, and the Quest for the Ultimate Theory.* New York: Vintage Books, 2000.

___. *The Fabric of the Cosmos: Space, Time, and the Texture of Reality.* New York: Knopf, 2004.

Greenfield, Susan A. *Journey to the Centers of the Mind: Toward a Science of Consciousness.* New York: W.H. Freeman, 1995.

Gribbon, John. *In Search of Schrödinger's Cat: Quantum Physics and Reality.* New York: Bantam, 1984.

___. *Schrödinger's Kittens and the Search for Reality.* New York: Back Bay Books, 1996.

Grof, Stanislav, and Hal Zina Bennett. *The Holotropic Mind: The Three Levels of Human Consciousness and How They Shape Our Lives.* New York: HarperCollins, 1993.

Hameroff, Stuart R. *Ultimate Computing: Biomolecular Consciousness and Nanotechnology.* Amsterdam: North Holland, 1987.

Hawking, Stephen. *The Universe in a Nutshell.* New York: Bantam Books, 2001.

Herbert, N. *Elemental Mind: Human Consciousness and the New Physics.* New York: Dutton, 1993.

Ho, Mae-Wan. *The Rainbow and the Worm. The Physics of Organisms.* Singapore: World Scientific, 1999.

Hunt, Valerie V. *Infinite Mind: Science of Human Vibrations of Consciousness.* Malibu, CA: Malibu Publishing, 2000.

Jahn, Robert G., and Brenda J. Dunne. *Margins of Reality: The Role of Consciousness in the Physical World.* London: Harcourt Brace Jovanovich, 1987.

Johnson, Steven. *Mind Wide Open: Your Brain and the Neuroscience of Everyday Life.* New York: Scribner, 2004.

Kaku, Michio. *Hyperspace: A Scientific Odyssey Through Parallel Universes, Time Warps and the Tenth Dimension*. New York: Anchor, 1995.

___. *Visions: How Science Will Revolutionize the 21st Century*. New York: Anchor Books, 1998.

Katra, Jane and Russell Targ. *The Heart of the Mind: How to Experience God Without Belief*. Novato, CA: New World Library, 1999.

Krishnamurti, Jiddu, *The Ending of Time*: J. Krishnamurti and Dr. David Bohm. San Francisco: HarperSan Franicsco, 1985.

Krueger, Myron. *Artificial Reality 2*. Reading, MA: Addison-Wesley, 1991.

Kurzweil, Ray. *The Age of Spiritual Machines: When Computers Exceed Human Intelligence*. New York: Penguin, 1999.

Lacerra, Peggy, and Roger Bingham. *The Origin of Minds: Evolution, Uniqueness, and the New Science of the Self*. New York: Harmony, 2002.

Lawlor, Robert. *Sacred Geometry, Philosophy and Practice*. London: Thames and Hudson Ltd., 1982.

Laszlo, Erwin. *The Creative Cosmos: A Unified Science of Matter, Life and Mind*. Edinburgh, Scotland: Floris Books, 1996.

___. *The Interconnected Universe: Conceptual Foundations of Transdisciplinary Unified Theory*: Singapore: World Scientific, 1995.

Le Shan, Lawrence. *The Medium, the Mystic, and the Physicist: Toward a General Theory of the Paranormal*. New York: Penguin USA, 1995.

___. *Clairvoyant Reality*. Wellingborough, Northants: Turnstone, 1982.

Lee, R.H. *Bioelectric Vitality: Exploring the Science of Human Energy*. San Clemente, CA: China Healthways Institute, 1997.

Livio, Mario. *The Golden Ratio: The Story of PHI, the World's Most Astonishing Number*. New York: Broadway, 2003.

Loye, David. *An Arrow Through Chaos: How We See into the Future*. Rochester, VT: Inner Traditions, 2000.

Mansfield, Victor. *Head and Heart: A Personal Exploration of Science and the Sacred*. Wheaton, IL: Quest Books, 2000.

McKibben, Bill. *Enough: Staying Human in an Engineered Age*. New York: Owl Books, 2004.

McMoneagle, Joseph. *Mind Trek: Exploring Consciousness, Time and Space through Remote Viewing*. Charlottesville, VA: Hampton Roads, 1993.

___. *The Ultimate Time Machine: a Remote Viewer's Perception of Time, and Predictions for the New Millennium*. Charlottesville, VA: Hampton Roads, 1998.

McTaggart, Lynne. *The Field: The Quest for the Secret Force of the Universe*. New York: HarperCollins, 2002.

Mandelbrot, Benoit B. *The Fractal Geometry of Nature*. New York: W.H. Freeman & Co., 1982.

Manning, Jeane. *The Coming Energy Revolution: The Search for Free Energy*. Garden City Park, NY: Avery, 1996.

Mansfield, Victor. *Synchronicity, Science, and Soul-Making*. Chicago IL: Open Court, 1995.

Meyer, Christopher, and Stan Davis. *It's Alive: The Coming Convergence of Information, Biology, and Business*. New York: Crown Business, 2003.

Mindell, Arnold. *Quantum Mind: The Edge Between Physics & Psychology*. Portland, OR: Lao Tse Press, 2000.

Mitchell, Edgar, and Dwight Williams. *The Way of the Explorer: An Apollo Astronaut's Journey Through the Material and Mystical Worlds*. New York: Putnam, 1996.

Mulhall, Douglas. *Our Molecular Future: How Nanotechnology, Robotics, Genetics, and Artificial Intelligence Will Transform Our World.* New York: Prometheus, 2002.

Negroponte, Nicholas. *Being Digital.* New York: Vintage Books, 1995.

Peat, F. David. *Blackfoot Physics: A Journey into the Native American Worldview.* Grand Rapids, MI: Phanes Pr; 2002.

____. *Synchronicity: The Bridge Between Matter and Mind.* New York: Bantam, 1987.

Peitgan, Heinz-Otto, H. Jürgens, and D. Saupe. *Chaos and Fractals: New Frontiers of Science.* New York: Springer Verlag, 1992.

Penrose, Roger. *Shadows of the Mind: A Search for the Missing Science of Consciousness.* London: Vintage, 1994.

Pinker, Steven. *How the Mind Works.* Hamondsworth: Penguin, 1998.

Prantzos, Nikos. *Our Cosmic Future: Humanity's Fate in the Universe.* New York: Cambridge University Press. 2000.

Pribram, Karl H. *Languages of the Brain: Experimental Paradoxes and Principles in Neuropsychology.* New York: Brandon House, 1982.

Radin, Dean I. *The Conscious Universe: The Scientific Truth of Psychic Phenomena.* New York: HarperEdge, 1997.

Rawles, Bruce. *Sacred Geometry Design Sourcebook: Universal Dimensional Patterns.* Nevada City, CA: Elysian Publishing, 1997.

Rheingold, Howard. *Virtual Reality: The Revolutionary Technology of Computer-Generated Artificial Worlds—and How It Promises to Transform Society.* New York: Touchstone, 1991.

Russell, Peter. *From Science to God: A Physicist's Journey into the Mystery of Consciousness.* Novato, CA: New World Library, 2003.

Schneider, Michael S. *A Beginner's Guide to Constructing the Universe: Mathematical Archetypes of Nature, Art, and Science*. New York: Harper Perennial, 1995.

Schiff, Michel. *The Memory of Water: Homeopathy and the Battle of Ideas in the New Science*. London: Thorsons, 1995.

Schrödinger, Erwin. *What Is Life?* New York: Cambridge University Press, 1992.

Schwartz, Gary E.R., and Linda G.S. Russek. *The Living Energy Universe: A Fundamental Discovery that Transforms Science & Medicine*. Charlottesville, VA: Hampton Roads, 1999.

Sheldrake, Rupert. *A New Science of Life: The Hypothesis of Morphic Resonance*. Rochester, VT: Park Street Press, 1995.

___. *The Rebirth of Nature: The Greening of Science and God*. Rochester, VT: Park Street Press, 1994.

___. *The Sense of Being Stared At And Other Unexplained Powers of the Human Mind*. New York: Three Rivers Press, 2004.

Singer, June. *Seeing Through the Visible World: Jung, Gnosis, and Chaos*. San Francisco: HarperSan Francisco, 1990.

Steiner, Rudolf. *The Fourth Dimension: Sacred Geometry, Alchemy, and Mathematics*. Trans. Catherine E. Creeger. Great Barrington, MA: Anthroposophic Press, 2001.

Strogatz, Steven. *Sync: The Emerging Science of Spontaneous Order*. New York: Hyperion, 2003.

Sutton, Daud. *Platonic & Archimedean Solids*. New York: Walker & Co., 1992.

Swann, Ingo. *Natural ESP*. New York: Bantam, 1987.

Talbot, Michael. *The Holographic Universe*. New York: Harper Collins, 1991.

___. *Mysticism and the New Physics*. New York: Arkana, 1993.

Targ, Russell. *Limitless Mind: A Guide to Remote Viewing and Transformation of Consciousness*. Novato, CA.New World Library, 2004.

Targ, Russell, and Jane Katra. *Miracles of Mind: Exploring Nonlocal Consciousness and Spiritual Healing*. Novato, CA: New World Library, 1999.

Targ, Russell, and Harold Puthoff. *Mind Reach: Scientists Look at Psychic Ability*. New York: Delacorte Press, 1977.

Tiller, William, Walter Dibble, and Michael Kohane. *Conscious Acts of Creation: The Emergence of the New Physics*. Walnut Creek, CA: Pavior, 2001.

Tiller, William A. *Science and Human Transformation: Subtle Energies, Intentionality and Consciousness*. Walnut Creek, CA: Pavior Publishing, 1997.

Toben, Bob. *Space-Time and Beyond: Toward an Explanation of the Unexplainable*. New York: Bantam, 1987.

Wade. David. *Li: Dynamic Form in Nature*. New York: Walker & Co., 2003.

Wade, Jenny. *Changes of Mind: A Holonomic Theory of the Evolution of Consciousness*. Albany, NY: State University of New York Press, 1996.

Walker, Evan Harris. *The Physics of Consciousness: The Quantum Mind and the Meaning of Life*. Cambridge, MA: Perseus Publishing, 2000.

Watson, Lyall. *The Nature of Things: The Secret Life of Inanimate Objects*. Rochester, VT: Destiny Books, 1992.

Wilber, Ken, ed. *The Holographic Paradigm and Other Paradoxes: Exploring the Leading Edge of Science*. Boulder, CO: Shambhala, 1982.

Wolf, Fred Alan. *Matter into Feeling: A New Alchemy of Science and Spirit*. Needham, MA: Moment Point Press, 2002.

___. *Mind Into Matter: A New Alchemy of Science and Spirit*. Needham, MA: Moment Point Press, 2000.

___. *Taking the Quantum Leap: The New Physics for Non-Scientists*. New York: HarperCollins, 1981.

Zajonc, Arthur. *Catching the Light: The Entwined History of Light and Mind*. New York: Oxford University Press, 1995.

Zohar, Danah. *The Quantum Self*. New York: Quill, 1991.

Zukav, Gary. *The Dancing Wu Li Masters: An Overview of the New Physics*. New York: Bantam, 1982.

Philosophy/Religion

Aïvanhov, Omraam Mikhaël. *Light Is a Living Spirit*. Colebrook, NH: Provsveta USA, 1987.

Amaringo, Pablo, and Luis Eduardo Luna. *Ayahuasca Visions: The Religious Iconography of a Peruvian Shaman*. Berkeley, CA: North Atlantic Books, 1999.

Angus S. *The Mystery-Religions: A Study in the Religious Background of Early Christianity*. Mineola, NY: 1975.

'Arabi, Ibn. *Journey to the Lord of Power: A Sufi Manual on Retreat*. Trans. Rabia Terry Harris. Rochester, VT: Inner Traditions, 1990.

Armstrong, Karen. *A History of God: The 4,000 Year Quest of Judaism, Christianity and Islam*. New York: Alfred A. Knopf, 1993.

Aurobindo, Sri. *The Essential Aurobindo*, ed. R. A. McDermott. 1973; reprint, Hudson, NY: Lindisfarne Press, 1987.

___. *The Mind of Light*. New York: Dutton, 1971.

Barnes, Trevor. *The Kingfisher Book of Religions: Festivals, Ceremonies, and Beliefs from Around the World*. New York: Kingfisher, 1999.

Bhagavad-Gita: The Song of God. Trans. Swami Prabhavananda, and Christopher Isherwood. New York: Signet Book, 2002.

Batchelor, Stephen. *Buddhism Without Beliefs: A Contemporary Guide to Awakening*. New York: Riverhead Books, 1997.

Bayman, Henry. *The Secret of Islam: Love and Law in the Religion of Ethics*. Berkeley, CA: North Atlantic Books, 2003.

Berg, Rav. *The Essential Zohar: The Source of Kabbalistic Wisdom*. New York: Bell Tower, 2002.

Blau, Evelyne. *Krisnamurti: 100 Years*. New York: Joost Elffers-Stewart, Tabori & Chang, 1995.

Blavatsky, Helen Petrovna. *The Secret Doctrine*. Pasadena, CA: Theosophical University Press, 1999.

Boissiere, Robert. *Meditations With the Hopi*. Santa Fe: Bear & Co., 1986.

Boorstein, Sylvia. *It's Easier Than You Think: The Buddhist Way to Happiness*. San Francisco: HarperSan Francisco, 1995.

Brach, Tara. *Radical Acceptance: Embracing Your Life With the Heart of a Buddha*. New York: Bantam, 2003.

Brown, Joseph E., ed. *The Sacred Pipe: Black Elk's Account of the Seven Rites of the Oglala Sioux*. Norman, OK: University of Oklahoma Press, 1953.

Bstan-'dzin-rgya-mtsho, Dalai Lama XIV. *Beyond Dogma: Dialogues and Discourses*. Berkeley, CA: North Atlantic Books, 1996.

___. *Essential Teachings*. Trans. Zélie Pollon, ed. Marianne Dresser. Berkeley, CA: North Atlantic Books, 1995.

Buber, Martin. *I and Thou*. Trans. R. G. Smith. 1923; reprint, New York: Charles Scriber & Sons, 1970.

___. *Tales of Hasidism: The Early Masters*. New York: Schocken Books, 1975.

Cahill, Thomas. *The Gifts of the Jews: How a Tribe of Desert Nomads Changed the Way Everyone Thinks and Feels*. New York: Nan A. Talese, 1998.

Caussade, Jean-Pierre de. *Abandonment to Divine Providence*. Trans. John Beevers. New York: Image, 1993.

Chilton, Bruce. *Rabbi Jesus: An Intimate Biography*. New York: Doubleday, 2000.

Chittich, William C. *Sufism*. Oxford: Oneworld Publications, 2000.

Cleary, Thomas F. *Immortal Sisters: Secret Teachings of Taoist Women*. Berkeley, CA: North Atlantic Books, 1996.

Cooper, D. Jason. *Mithras: Mysteries and Initiation Rediscovered*. York Beach, ME: Samuel Weiser, 1996.

Corbin, Henry. *The Man of Light in Iranian Sufism*, trans. N. Pearson. New Lebanon, NY: Omega Publications, 1994.

A Course in Miracles: combined volume. Glen Ellen, CA: Foundation for Inner Peace, 1992.

Crane, Frank. *The Lost Books of the Bible and the Forgotten Books of Eden*. New York: New American Library, 1963.

Das, Surya. *Awakening the Buddha Within*. New York: Broadway Books, 1998.

De Mello, Anthony. *Awareness*. New York: Image Books, 1990.

The Dhammapada: The Sayings of the Buddha, rendering by Thomas Byrom. New York: Harmony/Bell Tower, 2001.

Diaz, Frank. *The Gospel of the Toltecs: The Life and Teachings of Quetzalcoatl*. Rochester, VT: Inner Traditions, 2002.

Douglas-Klotz, Neil. *Prayers of the Cosmos: Meditations on the Aramaic Words of Jesus*. New York: HarperSan Francisco, 1994.

Drosnin, Michael. *The Bible Code*. New York: Simon & Schuster, 1997.

Dupont-Sommer, André, *The Essene Writings From Qumran*. Trans. G. Vermes. Gloucester, MA: Peter Smith, 1973.

Eagle, Chokecherry Gall. *Beyond the Lodge of the Sun: Inner Mysteries of the Native American Way*. New York: Vega, 2003.

Easwaran, Eknath. *The Compassionate Universe*. Petaluma, CA: Nilgiri Press, 1989.

Eckhart, Meister. *Meister Ekhart: Selected Treatises and Sermons*, trans. J. M. Clark and J. V. Skinner. London: Faber & Faber, 1958.

Erickson, Erik H. *Gandhi's Truth: On the Origins of Militant Nonviolence*. New York: W. W. Norton, 1969.

Esposito, John. *Islam: The Straight Path*. New York: Oxford University Press, 1998.

The Essence of Self-Realization: The Wisdom of Paramhansa Yogananda. Comp. Kriyananda (J. Donald Walters). Nevada City, CA: Crystal Clarity Publishers, 1990.

Ewing, Upton. *The Prophet of the Dead Sea Scrolls*. Joshua Tree, CA: Tree of Life Publications, 1993.

Fox, Matthew. *The Coming of the Cosmic Christ*. San Francisco: Harper & Row, 1988.

Freemantle, Francesca, and Chögyam Trungpa. *The Tibetan Book of the Dead*. Boston: Shambhala, 1975.

Garrett, Michael. *Walking on the Wind: Cherokee Teachings for Harmony and Balance*. Santa Fe, NM: Bear & Co., 1998.

Gold, Tara. *Open Your Mind, Open Your Life: A Book Of Eastern Wisdom*. Kansas City, MO: Andrews McMeel Publishing, 2002.

Goldsmith, Joel S. *Spiritual Interpretation of Scripture*. Camarillo, CA: DeVorss, 1983.

Govinda, Anagarika. *Foundations of Tibetan Mysticism*. New York: Weiser, 1969.

Hariharananda Aranya, Swami. *Yoga Philosophy of Patanjali*. Calcutta: University of Calcutta, 2000.

Hixon, Lex. *Mother of the Universe: Vision of the Goddess and Tantric Hymns of Enlightenment*. Wheaton, IL: Quest Books, 1994.

Holl, Adolf. *The Left Hand of God: A Biography of the Holy Spirit*. New York: Doubleday, 1998.

Holmes, Ernest. *The Science of Mind*. Los Angeles: Jeremy P. Tarcher, 1998.

Holy Bible: Authorized King James Version. Grand Rapids, MI: World Publishing, 1989.

The Holy Qur'an, trans. and commentary Maulana Muhammad Ali. Columbus, OH: Ahmadiyyah Anjuman Isha'at Islam Lahore, 1995.

Horsley, Richard A. and Neil Asher Silberman. *The Message of the Kingdom: How Jesus and Paul Ignited a Revolution and Transformed the Ancient World*. New York: Grosset-Putnam, 1997.

James, William. *The Varieties of Religious Experience*. New York: Collier Books, 1961.

Jenkins, John Major. *Galactic Alignment: The Transformation of Consciousness According to Mayan, Egyptian and Vedic Traditions*. Rochester, VT: Inner Traditions, 2002.

John of the Cross, Saint. *Dark Night of the Soul*. Trans and ed. E. Allison Peers. Garden City, NY: Image Books, 1959.

Johnson, Will. *Rumi: Gazing at the Beloved: The Radical Practice of Beholding the Divine*. New York: Inner Traditions, 2003.

Jordan, Michael. *Encyclopedia of Gods: Over 2,500 Deities of the World*. New York: Facts on File, 1993.

Krisnamurti, Jiddu. *Think On These Things*. New York: Perennial, 1989.

Kwong, Jakusho. *No Beginning, No End: The Intimate Heart of Zen*, New York: Harmony, 2003.

Lamsa, George M. *Gospel Light: An Indispensable Guide to the Teachings of Jesus and the Customs of His Time*. San Francisco: HarperSan Francisco, 1986.

The Layman's Parallel Bible: Comparing Four Popular Translations in Parallel Columns. Grand Rapids: Zondervan Corporation, 1973.

Leet, Leonora. *The Kabbalah of the Soul: The Transformative Psychology and Practices of Jewish Mysticism.* Rochester, VT: Inner Traditions, 2003.

Lings, Martin. *Muhammad: His Life Based on the Earliest Sources.* Rochester, VT: Inner Traditions, 1983.

Mack, Burton L. *The Lost Gospel: The Book of Q and Christian Origins.* New York: Harper SanFrancisco, 1994.

Maharaj, Nisargadatta. *I Am That.* Bombay, India: Chetana, 1973.

Maharshi, Ramana. *Spiritual Teachings.* Boulder, CO: Shambala, 1972.

Mails, Thomas E., and Dan Evehema. *Hotevilla: Hopi Shrine of the Covenant.* New York: Marlowe & Co., 1995.

Marion, Jim. *Putting on the Mind of Christ: The Inner Work of Christian Spirituality.* Charlottesville, VA: Hampton Roads, 2002.

Maslow, Abraham. *Religions, Values and Peak Experiences.* Cleveland, OH: State Univ. of Ohio, 1964.

Mattern, Evelyn. *Why Not Become Fire?* Notre Dame, IN: Ave Maria Press, 1999.

Men, Hunbatz. *Secrets of Mayan Science/Religion.* Santa Fe, NM: Bear & Co., 1990.

Merton, Thomas. *No Man Is an Island.* San Diego, CA: Harvest Books, 2002.

Miller, John, and Aaron Kenedi, eds. *God's Breath: Sacred Scriptures of the World.* New York: Marlowe & Co., 2000.

Montejo, Victor. *Popol Vuh: A Sacred Book of the Maya.* Trans. David Unger. Buffalo, NY: Douglas and McIntyre, 1999.

Neihardt, John G. *Black Elk Speaks: Being the Life Story of a Holy Man of the Oglala Sioux.* 1932; reprint, Lincoln: University of Nebraska Press, 1988.

Nh'ât Hahn, Thích. *Creating True Peace: Ending Violence in Yourself, Your Family, Your Community and the World.* New York: Free Press, 2003.

___. *Living Buddha, Living Christ.* New York: Riverhead Books, 1995.

___. *Zen Keys: A Guide to Zen Practice.* New York: Image, 1995.

Nikhilananda, Swami, trans., *The Gospel of Sri Ramakrishna*, abridged ed. New York: Ramakrishna-Vivekananda Center, 1970.

Novak, Philip. *The World's Wisdom: Sacred Texts of the World's Religions.* San Francisco: Harper SanFrancisco, 1995.

Occhiogrosso, Peter. *The Joy of Sects: A Spirited Guide to the World's Religious Traditions.* New York: Image, 1996.

O'Donohue, John. *Anam Cara: A Book of Celtic Wisdom.* New York: Harper-Collins, 1997.

Osborne, Arthur. *Ramana Maharshi and the Path of Self-Knowledge.* New York: Samuel Weiser, 1970.

Pagels, Elaine. *Beyond Belief: The Secret Gospel of Thomas.* New York: Random House, 2003.

___. *The Gnostic Gospels.* New York: Vintage Books, 1979.

The Philokalia: The Complete Text. Palmer, G.E.H., Philip Sherrard, and Kallistos Ware, eds. and trans. New York: Faber & Faber, 1999.

Po, Huang, *The Zen Teachings of Huang Po: On the Transmission of Mind.* Trans. J. Blofield. New York: Grove Weidenfeld, 1958.

Rahula, Walpola. *What the Buddha Taught*. New York: Grove Press, 1959.

Ranganath, S. *Rig Veda and Its Importance*. Bangalore:Indian Institute of World Curture, 1988.

Rilke, Rainer Maria. *Rilke's Book of Hours: Love Poems to God*. Trans. Anita Barrows and Joanna Macy. New York: Riverhead Books, 1996.

Robinson, James M., ed. *The Nag Hammadi Library in English*. New York: Harper & Row, 1977.

Robinson, Richard H., and Willard L. Johnson. *The Buddhist Religion: A Historical Introduction*. 3rd ed. Belmont, CA: Wadsworth, 1982.

Rumi, Jelaluddin. *The Essential Rumi*. Trans. Coleman Barks, with John Moyne, A. J. Arberry, and Reynold Nicholson. San Francisco: HarperSan Francisco, 1995.

___. *The Ruins of the Heart*. Trans. Edmund Helminski. Putney, VT: Threshold, 1981.

Rushkoff, Douglas. *Nothing Sacred: The Truth About Judaism*. New York: Three Rivers Press, 2004.

Salzberg, Sharon. *Faith: Trusting Your Own Deepest Experience*. New York: Riverhead, 2002.

___. *A Heart as Wide as the World: Stories on the Path of Lovingkindness*. Boston: Shambhala, 1997.

___. *Lovingkindness: The Revolutionary Art of Happiness*. Boston: Shambhala, 1995.

Sepher Yetzirah: The Book of Creation. Ed. Aryeh Kaplan. York Beach, ME: Samuel Weiser, 1997.

Sidharth, B. G. *The Celestial Key to the Vedas: Discovering the Origins of the World's Oldest Civilization*. Rochester, VT: Inner Traditions, 1999.

Shanks, Hershel. *The Mystery and Meaning of the Dead Sea Scrolls*. New York: Random House, 1998.

Sharma, Arvind. *Our Religions: The Seven World Religions Introduced by Preeminent Scholars from Each Tradition.* San Francisco: HarperSan Francisco, 1993.

Singh, Darshan. *The Wonders of Inner Space: Mystic Talks.* Bowling Green, VA: Sawan Kirpal Pulications, 1988.

Smith, Huston. *The World's Religions: Our Great Wisdom Traditions.* San Francisco: Harper SanFrancisco, 1999.

Smith, Huston, and Philip Novak. *Buddhism: A Concise Introduction.* San Francisco: HarperSan Francisco, 2003.

Sogyal, Rinpoche. *The Tibetan Book of Living and Dying.* New York: HarperSan Francisco, 1994.

Starbird, Margaret. *The Feminine Face of Christiantity.* Wheaton, IL: Quest, 2003.

Storm, Hyemeyohsts. *Seven Arrows.* New York: Ballantine Books, 1972.

Strong, Mary, ed. *Letters of the Scattered Brotherhood.* San Francisco: HarperSan Francisco, 1991.

Swedenborg, Emanuel. *Heaven and Hell.* New York: Swendenborg Foundation, 1984.

The Talmud: The Steinsaltz Edition. commentary Adin Steinsaltz. New York: Random House, 1989.

Teasdale, Wayne. *The Mystic Heart: Discovering a Universal Spirituality in the World's Religions.* Novato, CA: New World Library, 2001.

Teresa, of Avila, Saint. *Interior Castle.* Trans. E. Allison Peers. Garden City, NY: Image Books, 1972.

Teresa, Mother. *One Heart Full of Love.* Ann Arbor, MI: Servant Publications, 1988.

___. *A Simple Path.* Comp. Lucinda Vardey. New York: Ballantine, 1995.

Tillich, Paul. *Dynamics of Faith.* New York: Harper & Row, 1957.

Tzu, Lao. *Tao Te Ching,* trans. Stephen Mitchell. New York: Harper Perennial, 2000.

Uhlein, Gabriele, trans. *Meditations with Hildegarde von Bingen*. Santa Fe, NM: Bear & Co., 1982.

Upanishads, Breath of the Eternal. Trans. Swami Prabhavananda, and Frederick Manchester. Hollywood, CA. Vedanta Press, 1971.

Walvoord, John F. *Every Prophecy of the Bible*. Colorado Springs, CO: Chariot Victor Publishing, 1999.

Watts, Alan. *Behold the Spirit: A Study in the Necessity of Mystical Religion*. New York: Vintage, 1972.

Weeks, Andrew. *German Mysticism from Hildegard of Bingen to Ludwig Wittgenstein*. Albany, NY: State University of New York Press, 1993.

Wilcox, Joan Parisi. *Keepers of the Ancient Knowledge: The Mystical World of the Q'ero Indians of Peru*. New York: Sterling, 2002.

Winkler, Gershon. *Magic of the Ordinary: Recovering the Shamanic in Judaism*. Berkeley, CA: North Atlantic Books, 2003.

Yogananda, Paramhansa. *Whispers From Eternity*. Los Angeles, CA: Self Realization Fellowship, 1959.

Permissions

Let's Stay Connected

You are invited to share your questions, comments, feelings and stories. Please visit us at:

www.radiantstarpublishing.com

If you prefer to correspond via the postal service, please write to:

Radiant Star Publishing

P. O. Box 160

Carlton, WA 98814-0160